Revision Strategies
for Adolescent Writers

In memory of Donald Graves (1930—2010), a dear friend, mentor, and colleague who taught us to be writers and teachers of writing.

To all my students whose writings inspired me to write this book.
JAB

To my parents Ed and Dorna, and to my brother Dan—for lessons in revising life.
DH

To PR for unconditional love and guidance.
SR

Revision Strategies
for Adolescent Writers

Moving Students in the *Write* Direction

Jolene Borgese
Dick Heyler
Stephanie Romano
Foreword by Vickie Spandel

CORWIN
A SAGE Company

CORWIN
A SAGE Company

FOR INFORMATION:

Corwin

A SAGE Company

2455 Teller Road

Thousand Oaks, California 91320

(800) 233-9936

Fax: (800) 417-2466

www.corwin.com

SAGE Ltd.

1 Oliver's Yard

55 City Road

London EC1Y 1SP

United Kingdom

SAGE India Pvt. Ltd.

B 1/I 1 Mohan Cooperative Industrial Area

Mathura Road, New Delhi 110 044

India

SAGE Asia-Pacific Pte. Ltd.

33 Pekin Street #02-01

Far East Square

Singapore 048763

Acquisitions Editor: Carol Chambers Collins

Associate Editor: Megan Bedell

Editorial Assistant: Sarah Bartlett

Production Editor: Amy Schroller

Copy Editor: Cate Huisman

Typesetter: C&M Digitals (P) Ltd.

Proofreader: Jeff Bryant

Indexer: Maria Sosnowski

Cover Designer: Karine Hovsepian

Permissions Editor: Adele Hutchinson

Copyright © 2012 by Corwin

Printed in the United States of America

Library of Congress Cataloging-in-Publication Data

Borgese, Jolene.

Revision strategies for adolescent writers: moving students in the write direction/Jolene Borgese, Dick Heyler, Stephanie Romano; foreword by Vickie Spandel.

p.cm.

Includes bibliographical references and index.

ISBN 978-1-4129-9425-5 (paper)

1. English language—Composition and exercises—Study and teaching (Secondary) I. Heyler, Dick. II. Romano, Stephanie. III. Title.

LB1631.B735 2012

808'.0420712—dc23   2011039019

This book is printed on acid-free paper.

11 12 13 14 15 10 9 8 7 6 5 4 3 2 1

Contents

Foreword

This isn't just another book about teaching writing. It's a book about teaching *revision:* the very heart and soul of good writing. The sine qua non. Or to put it another way, until we teach revision, we're not really teaching writing at all. In *Revision Strategies,* authors Jolene Borgese, Dick Heyler, and Stephanie Romano take us on a virtual tour through the world of revision. They share lessons that will engage students, but more important, allow them to see their writing change right before their eyes. When that happens, students sense—some for the first time—that they truly *are* writers. There's a word for that feeling: success.

In the thousands of writing workshops I've conducted, the question I've most often asked teachers is this: *What is the most challenging part of writing to teach?* Almost to a teacher they say revision, revision . . . *revision.* And no wonder, for revision is an art. Consider *why* writers revise: to clarify meaning, sharpen voice, or touch a reader's heart. Such changes demand insight and strategy—and these are not simple things to teach.

That's precisely where this book comes in. It's a collection of strategies, yes—but strategies designed to build understanding. Anyone can toss together a random collection of lessons. But lessons that take writers deep inside their own writing and help them understand how revision works are rare. That's what makes this carefully selected collection so special; it pays homage to the true nature of revision by giving young writers the skills and guidance they need to see their work with new eyes—more as an editor might see it.

You can bet that any genuinely thoughtful book on revision captures my attention. After all, I've been working with 6-Trait writing since the mid-1980s, way back when Beaverton's extraordinary teacher team developed the first 6-Trait model. Though our original focus was on writing assessment, it became apparent almost overnight that the real destiny of the 6-Traits was to influence *revision.* Trait-based instruction lays the groundwork for revision by showing writers what makes their writing work—or stands in the way. Now, with a fresh perspective, *Revision Strategies* links lessons in revision directly and clearly to *specific* traits. And those links make the underlying purpose behind every lesson clear: to help students revise for clarity, fluency, voice, detail, wording, idea development—and much more.

As you page through this book, here are just a few of the things you will notice—and love: First, these lessons make revision *fun.* This is no small achievement, because as anyone who has ever taught writing will tell you, many students dread revision. It just feels so . . . heavy, tedious, endless, and dull. Like relocating pyramids. As these authors remind us, to teach revision well we need to lighten up. We need to remind students that revision begins with sharing your opinion, your personal vision of which words sound right and which don't. Try it. Hand students colored pencils and turn them loose on a rough draft—and watch a classroom spring to life as formerly passive students morph into experts, passionate about writing, eager to transform a voiceless piece into something that could sway minds or capture hearts. When students feel that kind of power, revision is no longer a mindless chore; it's gamesmanship, choreography, design—and the options are *exciting.*

You'll also notice a strong emphasis on literature—on reading to become a writer. I applaud this with my whole being. Many years ago, I heard Don Graves (to whom this book is dedicated) say, "Writing is the making of reading." Think about this. Each time we write, we need to picture someone reading what we've written, and ask, *Will this make sense to that reader? Will he or she hear my voice?* And if the answer to either question is *no,* we have to try again—and again. Until it works. As writers, we don't *want* to give up once we believe someone is actually *listening.* We want to get the phrasing and the cadence just right—so we can connect with that someone waiting on the other side of our words. Good literature shows us how to do this; it's filled with examples of enticing leads, powerful voice, strong verbs, just right endings, and more. Throughout this book, well-loved authors like Jerry Spinelli and Gordon Korman share delightful bits of wisdom about their own writing processes. And in addition, the authors recommend numerous books to which we can turn when we want to show students how to develop ideas or organize details or write to persuade.

Though every lesson is a little different, you'll find the fabric of writing process and workshop woven all through this text. Leaf through the book to rediscover the impact of modeling, sharing aloud, conferring, working with peers, and interacting with text—searching out sensory details, finding that spot where an image or example would open things up for readers, highlighting verbs that work or clichés that don't. *Every lesson* packs a revision punch. And every lesson is designed to fit into the viable, fluid context of writers working with writers—because that's how coaches are made. A number of lessons are genre specific, designed to help students craft stronger examples of memoir, essays, poems, arguments, or other forms. This is particularly important not just because genre is an inherent component of both the Common Core Standards and the NCTE bedrock beliefs, but because clarity and voice stem from purpose. And genre is all about purpose. Once a writer knows *why* he or she is writing—to entertain, to teach, to convince—generalities dissolve like fog in the sun.

Maya Angelou once observed, "Some critics will write 'Maya Angelou is a natural writer'—which is right after being a natural heart surgeon." I love that. It's a wonderful and humorous reminder that writing is very hard work—for everyone—and make no mistake: Revision can be the hardest part. But revision is also joyful, rewarding, wondrous, freeing—and terribly important. A book like this matters because it teaches us, along with our students, how to do something that is both challenging and constructive. It teaches us to build bridges, writer to reader. Thank you, Jolene, Dick, and Stephanie, for sharing so many lessons that can make us all look and feel like "naturals."

Vicki Spandel
Author
The 9 Rights of Every Writer (2005)
Creating Young Writers, 3rd edition (2012)
Creating Writers, 6th edition (2013)

Acknowledgments

Many supportive hands have made this journey a reality! Our thanks and gratitude go out to the following people for their dedication, support, and enthusiasm for our project.

Our heartfelt gratitude to Dr. Maureen McLaughlin, East Stroudsburg University's Department of Reading Education chair, for her unfailing support. A special thanks to graduate assistants Chrissy Godiska, Nancy Sunn, Jackie Ackerman, Katie Lime, Nick Years, and Michele Pavesi for researching, reading, and formatting our manuscript. Thanks to the students in Stephanie's ESU classes who learned the revision strategies in class and then gave us valuable feedback with suggestions! A very special thank you to Jason Giandomenico, who brainstormed titles for us.

We are especially grateful to Sarah Lucci, one of Stephanie's graduate students and a teacher at South Mountain Middle School in Allentown, Pennsylvania, who invited us into her summer school class to work with her students and engaged her students throughout the school year in many of our frontloading activities and revision strategies. We also appreciate the students from Mrs. Batt's and Mr. Mell's high school writing classes in the Stroudsburg Area School District who provided us with writing samples.

A special thank you to all the teachers in Jolene's writing workshops and conferences, especially those at the Annual Keystone State Reading Association Conference, whose responses about revision became the bases for this book. Thank you for your honesty and support!

A special thanks to the teachers involved in the summer writing session of the Endless Mountains Writing Project at Mansfield University, who responded to many of our ideas and activities. The National Writing Project is the common denominator we have with them; it was profound to share this experience with other writing project teachers.

A special thank you also to Dick's students at Harlan Rowe Junior High School in the Athens Area School District in Athens, Pennsylvania, who participated in peer conferencing and in meaningful revision strategies during their writing workshops; they have contributed ideas and writing samples.

We are truly grateful to Nanci Werner-Burke, codirector with Dick of the Endless Mountains Writing Project at Mansfield University, for her expertise and revision strategy contributions in the digital communications section. We also appreciate the teacher perspectives of Alexandria Gibb, Heather Bresnick, and Rebecca Leitzell. We are indebted to Bethann McCain for enlightening us on digital communication.

A dear friend of Jolene's, Carolyn Smith, who was Jolene's English department chair at West Chester East High School, read and edited our manuscript many times. We appreciate her dedication and expertise. Dick's friend, Rick Greene, also read and gave suggestions for revisions on many of our chapters, and we are grateful for his time and support. Thanks to Dick's friend, Mike Kroeck, for his support and listening through the process.

A special thank you to our team at Corwin who helped us along our journey, especially our senior editor, Carol Collins, whose dedication supported us from the initial manuscript to its publication. Thank you to both Megan Bedell and Sarah Bartlett at Corwin who coached us through "dropbox," the journey of submitting a manuscript!

Finally, heartfelt gratitude to Mark Hansen, formerly of Corwin, who believed in us from the beginning and made this book possible.

Publisher's Acknowledgments

Corwin gratefully acknowledges the contributions of the following reviewers:

David Freitas, Professor, School of
   Education
Indiana University
South Bend, IN

Jamie Jahnig, English Teacher
Cheyenne Central High School
Cheyenne, WY

Brian T. Kissel, Assistant Professor,
   Reading and Elementary Education
University of North Carolina at Charlotte
Charlotte, NC

Sandy Moore, English Teacher
Coupeville High School
Coupeville, WA

Maryann Mraz, Associate Professor,
   Reading and Elementary Education
University of North Carolina at Charlotte
Charlotte, NC

Denise E Mullen, Social Studies
   Department Chair
James Monroe Middle School
Corrales, NM

Rebecca Rupert , English Teacher
Aurora Alternative High School
Bloomington, IN

Earl Squyres, English Teacher
Jackson Hole High School
Jackson, WY

Joseph Staub, Teacher, Resource
   Specialist
Thomas Starr King Middle School
Los Angeles, CA

Deborah Teitelbaum, Center Fellow
North Carolina Center for the
   Advancement of Teaching
Cullowhee, NC

Kristina Turner, English Teacher
T. L. Hanna High School
Anderson, SC

Stephen Valentine, Assistant Head
Upper School at Montclair Kimberley
   Academy
Montclair, NJ

Jeri H. Watts, Assistant Professor, School
   of Education and Human Development
Lynchburg College
Lynchburg, VA

About the Authors

The National Writing Project opened up the possibilities of writing for Jolene (center), Stephanie (right), and Dick (left), and now they are reaching their destination.

Jolene Borgese's experiences came from the fact that she was a young, naïve teacher with little writing instruction and experience. The remedy: She became involved in the first writing project in Pennsylvania in the summer of 1980 when she attended the first summer writing institute at West Chester University. For the next 15 years, she was the codirector of the project with Dr. Robert Weiss. Jolene taught writing strategies courses, designed the Summer Youth Writing Project, and went off site to lead summer institutes in different parts of the state. This life-changing event shaped her teaching, her career, and most importantly her students' learning.

She taught middle and high school for 21 years in suburban Philadelphia and earned her doctorate at Widener University, where she researched what made students successful on local, state, and national writing assessments. She left the classroom to work with teachers as a staff developer, a national 6-Traits trainer for a large educational publishing company. With a volunteer group, she traveled to Guatemala to help struggling schools. There she presented writing as a process, the 6 Traits, and frontloading strategies to Guatemalan teachers. All were eager and excited to learn about writing and methods to help their students be better writers. Jolene found that it didn't matter that most of the teachers were Spanish speaking and needed an interpreter to understand her; what they heard were motivating ideas, explicit instruction, and the power of literacy that they could pass on to their students.

Presently, Jolene has added to her resume the title of literacy professor at local universities. She is active in many professional literacy organizations and was program cochair for the Keystone State Reading Association annual conference that was held in October, 2011.

Dick Heyler's interest in writing and visualizing goes back to his college days at Penn State University, when he was a writing major with a minor in photography. After graduation, he traveled the country in Kerouac mode, working as a photographer.

From Maine to Colorado to Florida and every state in between, he met the people of the country and heard their stories.

Returning from the road, he began teaching English in the Athens Area School District in Athens, Pennsylvania. As his teaching shifted toward engaging his students in writing, he became more and more interested in the writing process, how the various elements interacted with each other, and how the same writing could grow. Now, 26 years after he began teaching, he is still a writing teacher for the Athens Area School District and codirector of the Endless Mountains Writing Project at Mansfield University. Dick believes writing is a solid way to tell our stories, and by our stories we understand our lives. He imparts this daily to his students. For him, this book is an invitation to learn and a journey for all teachers who teach writing.

Stephanie Romano taught first and second grade where creative writing was a part of the language arts curriculum. She encouraged her students to be storytellers and write their stories down, and through this authorship, both she and her students and school community heard and saw the power of their stories.

Years later, Stephanie was offered a position as a reading specialist in a public school in northeastern Pennsylvania. The school's administration asked her to gain knowledge in the writing process so she could meld the reading–writing connection for her at-risk students. She participated in the Pennsylvania Writing Project at West Chester University, where Jolene codirected the project. Through her writing experiences, she realized the reciprocal relationship: Writing is important to reading, and reading is important to writing. Over 20 years of working with at-risk readers and writers, she implemented the tools that her students needed to become more literate.

Stephanie was appointed to a statewide steering committee commissioned by the governor to develop the Oral History Project, an authentic learning experience integrating the academic standards of reading, writing, speaking, and listening. At the Governor's Institutes in Pennsylvania, this project was introduced to hundreds of teachers with the understanding that they would implement it in their classrooms. The project culminated in 2006 with the publishing of a book that Stephanie coauthored with colleagues Diane Skiffington Dickson, Dick Heyler, and Linda Reilly entitled *The Oral History Project: Connecting Students to Their Community, Grades 4–8.*

Stephanie is the past president of the Keystone State Reading Association and is presently the editor of their newsletter, *The Keystone Reader*. She earned her doctorate of education in reading at Lehigh University and has recently retired from the Department of Reading Education at East Stroudsburg University, Pennsylvania.

So, here we are today, writing together on our journey, yearning to help teachers share our passion for writing. Writing is careful thinking with intellectual responsibility. Our goal is to support teachers who in turn will move students in the ***Write Direction*** to use revision strategies meaningfully to become independent thinkers and writers.

Introduction

The Need for Revision Strategies

During Jolene's career as a writing project codirector and staff developer, she has asked thousands of teachers how they teach revision and what strategies they use to help students improve their initial drafts. At a recent workshop, thinking about our work on this book, Jolene asked the teachers to jot down their questions and comments about revision on 3 × 5 note cards. One teacher's response clearly recognizes the centrality of the revision process to good writing, while at the same time it acknowledges how difficult it is to teach revision:

> How can I teach revision effectively so my students become independent thinkers and writers?

It is this question—how to teach revision effectively, and particularly with adolescent writers—that lies at the heart of this book.

Other responses Jolene collected at the workshop reflect some common misconceptions about revision:

> How do you teach students to find mistakes?

> Where do you start to revise with some of your "worst" writers?

> How much does a student have to revise?

> How can I get students to recognize their errors?

The misconceptions these questions reveal are barriers to effective revision and are, unfortunately, prevalent in today's classrooms. They include the beliefs that

- the current atmosphere of testing does not allow for revision as part of writing instruction.
- editing and revision are the same.
- there is not enough time to teach revision and cover the rest of the curriculum.

These widely held misconceptions point to the need for teachers to gain more knowledge of and experience with the revision process and to benefit from the experiences of others. Hence this book: a collection of instructional revision strategies that teachers and students can implement during the writing process, selecting those that best meet their needs. Some of these revision strategies are uniquely ours, while others have been adapted from or inspired by the work of prestigious teachers of writing.

The 36 strategies in this book are designed for teachers' use as they instruct students how to think through the revision process. The strategies reflect the wisdom of teachers and students who successfully use the writing process as their framework for writing, thinking, and learning, and whose classroom interactions give witness to their understanding of the recursive and dynamic process of revision. The strategies include and demonstrate teachers' use of the following practices:

- Frontloading with familiarity and ease; that is, having students plan, rehearse, and converse during the prewriting stage, which, in turn, streamlines their writing as well as their revision process.
- Having students confer with peers during writers' workshop, to help them gather more ideas to incorporate into their revisions.
- Using technology as a means to give students multiple ways to collaborate and revise in and out of the classroom.
- Modeling effective revision strategies for their students, because teachers are writers as well as teachers of writing.

This book will be useful for teachers to strengthen their repertoire of revision strategies for effective instruction; the strategies may also be internalized by their students as the students become more fluent and confident writers. The strategies are designed to be flexible so that they can be taught numerous times and in many content areas.

Revision Throughout the Writing Process

No one writes perfectly the first time, no matter how experienced the writer may be; thoughtful and meaningful revisions are a natural part of the writing process. As Donald Murray wrote, "Revision is based on re-seeing the entire piece of writing" (Murray, 1995, p. xiv).

If we want our students to be better writers, they must see the positive effects of revision in the writing process. When students experience the modeling of effective strategies, implement these strategies with guidance, and reflect on their process of revision, they gain the confidence to improve their writing.

As teachers, we are aware that writing is a highly complex, cognitive process. "In order to compose or write, students must combine all their knowledge of the topic with their knowledge of the mechanics of language" (Borgese, 1998, p. 62). In addition, students need to hone their craft and hear their own voices to create meaningful revisions that ultimately improve the quality of their writing. Craft is the process of shaping and reshaping our material into a finished product, with an ideal reader in mind. This may be a "long, painstaking, patient process" (Graves, 1983, p. 6) that a writer endures until the final product is satisfying to the writer's purpose and audience. Our students need the same strategies and writing activities to compose and revise that professional writers experience during their writing process.

In the crafting of revision, the writer must not only read what is on the page, but must anticipate what is yet to be written. Writing is thinking, and sometimes the writer discovers something new or long forgotten (Murray, 1995). We have learned from the works of Murray and Graves that the writing process involves thinking that focuses both on the process and the product.

In the remainder of this introduction, before turning to the revision strategies themselves, we share some understandings about the writing process and revision that have grown out of many scholars' work in this field, and we share some reflections about a couple of current developments that are affecting the way we teach writing:

- The Process Approach
- Writer's Workshop
- Frontloading Activities
- The 6 Traits of Effective Writing
- Digital Communication
- The Common Core State Standards

The Process Approach

The recursive and dynamic nature of the writing process allows the writer to plan, draft, and revise, often all at the same time. The process approach, honed by Donald Graves (see Figure I.1), provides a guide for students and teachers as they develop their drafts.

When students begin with the reader in mind, writing becomes a complex mental activity. "Writing is where we learn to think" (Graves, 2004, p. 87). Putting thoughts and ideas into written words is an intellectual exercise that furthers thinking. When reading,

Figure I.1   Graves's process approach to writing and its implications for students and teachers.

The Process of Writing	Implications for Students	Implications for Teachers
Choice and rehearsal (prewriting)	Choice is motivating and empowering	Connect with our students and their interests
Composition (drafting)	Frontloading (rehearsal) gives students an opportunity to discover what they want to write	Guide students to research and choose their topics through frontloading activities
Voice (drafting)	Provides an opportunity to clarify ideas during writing	Guide students to develop organizational strategies

Guide students to develop their voices |
Conference (revising)	Write for appropriate purpose and audience	Provide time for meaningful feedback
Revision	Share writing with teacher and peers	Model peer revision strategies that help students to do further revision
Publishing	Bring clarity to the content	Model strategies to enhance clarity of content
	Share with an audience	Give the opportunity to be heard by authentic audiences

we retrieve ideas from our background knowledge to make connections and meaning. When writers use their background knowledge to create meaningful sentences, their readers interpret the meaning based on their own prior knowledge and experiences. Revision permeates the writing process but comes into play most prominently during the conference and revision stages.

Writers' Workshop

Nancie Atwell is the originator of writers' workshop, a now widely adopted practical application of the writing process for teachers and students. The workshop is where communities of writers work together to develop their skills and craft. It is during writers' workshop that students have opportunities to share their drafts with peers and rethink their writing as they prepare their final drafts for their readers.

Atwell designed writers' workshop with seven underlying principles that are listed in Figure I.2. The implementation of these principles is critical to making writers' workshop a successful and meaningful classroom practice.

Figure I.2 Atwell's seven underlying principles of writers' workshop.

Writers need regular chunks of time.

Writers need their own topics.

Writers need response.

Writers learn mechanics in context.

Writers need to know adults who write.

Writers need to read.

Writing teachers need to take responsibility for their knowledge and teaching.

Source: Atwell, 1987, pp. 17–18.

Within Atwell's writing workshop, there are four routines established: (1) the minilesson at the beginning of class, (2) writing workshop itself, where time is spent writing, (3) group share meeting during the last few minutes of class, and (4) the status-of-the-class conference, which begins after the first day. Revision strategies are often modeled by the teacher during the minilessons and practiced by the students during writing workshop time.

Frontloading

Revision actually begins before we start to write. Frontloading activities are executed during rehearsal, before any writing takes place. These activities help students to think about their ideas and how they might organize them. When frontloading is done thoughtfully, students often find that writing becomes easier, and the revisions needed are fewer.

Whereas prewriting is associated more with brainstorming ideas and details, frontloading involves selecting, prioritizing, and customizing. Frontloading activities may include creating visuals, making graphic organizers, collecting artifacts, role-playing, or responding to music. Frontloading is more than a word association web or cluster, more than making a list. It is thinking about the topic, about how to start a piece of writing or even how to end it. The writer performs frontloading activities, with multiple prewriting strategies, to develop ideas. Incorporating frontloading activities into the writing process shortens as well as strengthens the revision process. The revision strategies in Part II of this book all involve frontloading activities.

The right variety of frontloading activities will encourage, embrace, and extend the students' thinking to help them find the right topic, identify the right spin on the assignment, and provide substantial information. Complex prompts need more frontloading activities to provide students with ample information and alternative perspectives to incorporate into their writings. Just like athletes who run plays before the game, actors who rehearse their lines for a play, and painters who draw many sketches before they decide what to paint, student writers improve their work by engaging in a variety of frontloading activities.

6 Traits of Effective Writing

The 6 Traits of Effective Writing have given teachers a common vocabulary for instructional and assessment purposes. Using the results of Paul Diederich's research on the language of writing instruction and assessment, the 6 Traits model was developed in 1984 by a team of 17 teachers in Beaverton, Oregon, working under the direction of Vicki Spandel. Carol Meyer helped Vicki coordinate the team as director of assessment and evaluation for the Beaverton School District; she pulled the original team together and organized all the subsequent training of teachers that enabled us to field test the model with 5,000 Beaverton students while Vicki Spandel served as the scoring director.

The research model used in the development process was derived primarily from the work of Paul Diederich (*Measuring Growth in English*, 1974), and also from the work of Donald Murray (1982), who believed in and promoted a system of identifying the traits that make writing work in order to improve students' revision. His traits paralleled the 6 Traits very closely and both Diederich's and Murray's research inspired the development of the 6 Traits.

Many states have since integrated the 6 Traits of effective writing into their state frameworks. The revision strategies we offer are rooted in one or more of the 6 Traits of effective writing; their common language makes both teachers and students more confident when teaching, discussing, and assessing revision.

The 6 Traits and the writing process intersect and overlap as the semantic feature analysis chart shows in Figure I.3. As Culham points out, it is important that students be taught and understand the vocabulary that explains the writing process and that distinguishes revision from editing: "When . . . working with the idea, shaping it, rethinking it, and moving it forward . . . use the term *revision*. When . . . talking about cleaning up the text the way a copy editor would, then use the term *editing*" (2003, p. 25). When students are going through the revision process, they are attending to 5 of the 6 Traits (everything but the conventions that come into play during the editing process): ideas, organization, voice, word choice, and sentence fluency. It is essential to teach, model, and practice these traits of effective writing as students develop their drafts.

During the revision process, writers

- develop their ideas with interesting and important details.
- organize their drafts clearly and effectively.
- establish a voice that is a perfect match for their audience and purpose.
- use the most interesting and accurate words.
- construct phrases and **sentences** that enhance the intended meaning (Culham, 2003, p. 23).

Figure I.3   Connecting the writing process and the 6 Traits.

Writing Process/6 Traits	Ideas	Organization	Voice	Word Choice	Sentence Fluency	Conventions
Prewrite	•	•				
Draft	•	•	•			
Revision	•	•	•	•	•	
Edit						•

Source: greatsource.com/iwrite.

Because the 6 Traits are research-based and offer best practices for effective writing instruction, the revision strategies in this text have been correlated with the 6 Traits. On the first page of each part of the book, there is a chart that indicates which of the 6 Traits are involved in each of the strategies within that part.

Traits and Revision

The primary purpose of introducing the 6 Traits into the classroom is to strengthen revision—and editing skills. The first five traits—ideas, organization, voice, word choice, and sentence fluency—have traditionally been most closely connected with revision because, if you look closely at the top levels of any good writing guide, you see the very things writers do when they revise. They add detail or cut filler, reorder information or write a new lead, spice up voice, refine word choice, recraft sentences to smooth the flow. When we teach students the traits, we open a world of revision possibilities. The sixth trait, conventions, has always been linked to editing. After all, copy editors check punctuation, grammar and usage, spelling, and capitalization. Recent thinking has transformed this perspective in two ways.

First, conventions now also incorporate presentation: the layout within a written document—like a picture book or newspaper, or the style and overall flow of nontextual communication—such as a PowerPoint presentation or video. Second, with this expanded definition of conventions comes an understanding that conventions are not just about correctness; they also create and enhance both meaning and voice. To cite a few simple examples, think how paragraphing supports organization, how spelling clarifies word choice, how punctuation and italics show readers how to interpret dialogue. Because conventions do so much to support all the other traits, we are recognizing increasingly that editing has a role to play within the larger sphere of revision.

At the same time, we want students to make a distinction. Too many students see editing not as an integral part of revision, but as the whole of revision. This means they may correct spelling and insert missing punctuation and believe they have "revised" their work—when in fact they've barely touched the surface. We want to take students well beyond surface changes, giving them the skills they need to make big revisions: adding new information or beginning in a different way. In exploring such strategies, we'll be emphasizing the first five of the six traits and showing many connections to those five. But keep in mind that editing (tweaking conventions) or design (revamping the layout or presentation) can and will enhance any revision.

Source: Personal interview with Vicki Spandel, August 16, 2011.

Peer Response

Peer response helps students become more independent revisers. Whether reading, writing, speaking, or listening, all students are actively engaged during peer response in helping their fellow writers create better drafts, and in the process they develop a collection of strategies about how to respond to a text. Through playing the roles of writer, reader, and audience, students use critical reading, listening, and thinking skills as well as manners and empathy to fully respond to their peers' drafts. Writers have an audience to read to, an audience has the writers to respond to, and when combined, this peer conferencing process is an effective approach to guide writers through the revision process.

Digital Communication

The classroom is a place where tradition meets the latest innovative technology. Some districts are equipped with the latest computers, whiteboards, iPads, and document cameras; others have none of these technology tools. Even where these tools are available, some teachers fear the new and unknown and need professional development to understand it; others, often the digital natives among us, embrace the tools of digital communication that can motivate students and enhance their research, writing, and presenting skills.

Digital communication has made revision a much speedier and more efficient process. Adding information, removing information, moving information, or being more specific is as easy as a click on a keyboard. Because students are computer literate at such an early age, teachers need to give time and opportunities for students to compose, revise, and edit on the computer. There are many websites and programs that support students during the revision process. "The bottom line is that digital writing tools such as blogs, wikis, and collaborative word processors can enhance the writer's workshop" (Hicks, 2009, p. 36). The strategies in Part VII of this book sample the potential of some of these tools, demonstrating how they can be used effectively in the revision process.

Common Core State Standards (CCSS)

Finally, we turn our attention to the Common Core State Standards (CCSS) for English language arts. These guidelines support many of the elements we have incorporated into these chapters: the writing process, the three dominant text types, writers' workshop, peer response, and revision strategies in general. The CCSS acknowledge that components of the writing process—such as planning, drafting, revising, and editing—are applicable to the three text types in which students need to become proficient: narrative, information/explanatory, and argument. The major shift in CCSS with regard to writing is from persuasive text to the argument. In Part I of this book, revision strategies that incorporate frontloading activities, such as *Create an Argument*, provide students with a focused way to examine information that supports their positions. Teachers need to instruct students on how to create an argument that changes the reader's point of view, brings about some action on the reader's part, or asks the reader to accept a writer's explanation or evaluation of a concept, issue, or problem.

The CCSS writing standards for Grades 6–12 specify that students must "produce clear and coherent writing in which the development, organization, and style are appropriate to task, purpose, and audience" (www.corestandards.org). Part II of this book contains revision strategies that focus on ideas. By implementing these strategies, students strengthen ideas that are weak or underdeveloped in their drafts. The revision strategies in Part III address the organization of a draft. Part IV focuses on voice, word choice, and sentence fluency.

The CCSS language supports direct instruction of revision strategies and peer response during writers' workshop, stating that "with some guidance and support from peers and adults, students need to develop and strengthen writing as needed by planning, revising, and editing" (www.corestandards.org). Part V contains revision strategies that are fostered through peer conferences. Part VI offers strategies that rely on quality young adult literature to serve as mentor texts for examples and models that can be incorporated into students' writing.

The CCSS encourage *"the use of technology to produce and publish writing as well as to interact and collaborate with others"* (www.corestandards.org). The revision strategies in Part VII all incorporate digital communication. Students are adept at composing and revising on the computer, and there are many programs available to help students through the revision process. Realizing there are a plethora of sites available, we have featured as examples a few that have worked the best with our students.

PART I

Think From the Start:
Begin With Frontloading Activities

Words on Writing From Susan Campbell Bartoletti

It takes me at least two years to research and write a full-length nonfiction book. To write the "truth," writers must research to the edges of the story—and beyond. If we don't research to the edges, our story stays in the middle. The middle is where stereotypes live.

I begin my research by reading around, beginning with secondary sources. I pay close attention to footnotes, bibliographies, captions, and acknowledgments, because these things lead me to other important sources and collections housed in museums, historical societies, and academic libraries.

Research is time-consuming and some days I wonder if I'll ever know enough to begin writing. But if I begin to write too soon, before I feel ownership over the material, my writing will fall flat. It will be rendered voiceless, because I haven't breathed my own life into the story. That's what voice is, you know—breathing a story to life, giving the narrative the cadence and the rhythm that quickens the words and sentences to life. But worst of all, if I write too soon, I'll encounter writer's block, because, simply, I don't know enough.

On the other hand, research can become a sophisticated form of procrastination. And so, I know that when the facts repeat themselves, when I am no longer learning anything new, when I've found the story's cadence, it's time to begin writing.

As I write, I constantly double-check and triple-check facts. I also look for gaps, places where I need more information to flesh out the story. And so the research and writing processes continue, side-by-side. When I have finished the first draft, I outline what I've written, so that again, I can see gaps or places where I've repeated myself. An outline also helps me see—and improve—the story's shape.

P art I offers teachers strategies that use frontloading activities to enhance the revision process. Engaging in these activities before drafting encourages students to research their topics, thus gaining more information to write their drafts. Our premise is the more students think and talk about their topics and collect facts for their drafts, the fewer revisions they will need later in the process. Although we believe this to be true, these revision strategies are strong enough to be presented to students without frontloading activities.

In *Code the Text* and *Create an Argument,* for example, students are asked to analyze their drafts for clarity, and to add details and examples that will address their purpose and audience. The antithesis is true in *Cut, Slash, and Burn*, where students are required to delete chunks from their drafts that are not needed and do not focus on their purpose. In *Write an Effective Speech*, students are encouraged not only to analyze their speeches for organization but also to be keenly aware of their purpose and their audience, who will hear their speeches but not have the benefit of seeing them!

The Revision Strategies in Part I Correlated to the 6 Traits of Effective Writing

Strategy/6 Traits	Ideas	Organization	Voice	Word Choice	Sentence Fluency
Code the Text	•	•			
Cut, Slash, Burn	•	•	•		
Create a Character Sketch	•	•	•	•	
Create an Argument	•	•	•	•	
Write an Effective Speech	•	•	•	•	

Note: Since the revision strategies do not address Conventions, this trait is not represented in this chart.

1

Code the Text

Focus

Sometimes, students need to "see" what they have written. They have some clarity, descriptive details, and examples (C-D-E) already in their writing; it may be a good beginning draft, but more clarity, descriptive details, or examples would significantly improve the draft. By analyzing and coding the text, the students proceed to make C-D-E revisions (Spandel, 2009). Students code (preferably with three different colored pencils) their drafts where clarity, descriptive details, and examples already occur. Once they have highlighted their drafts, they know where more clarity, descriptive details, and examples are needed.

Definition

Clarity: Pieces of text that help the writer know that the text says exactly what he wants it to say; these words help the audience to have a clear understanding of the draft.

Descriptive Details: Pieces of text that the writer knows describe the draft well; these words help the audience to visualize the draft.

Examples: Pieces of text where the writer explains who, what, where, when, how, or why something is supportive to the text; these words give the audience additional information to make connections with the draft.

Frontloading Activity

Before writing their first draft of a personal narrative, the students in Miss Lucci's middle school class in an urban school were asked to listen to one of her favorite stories, *Wilfrid Gordon McDonald Partridge* by Mem Fox. They were asked to think about their memories as they listened. When the reading was completed, the students drew examples of their memories that corresponded to how a memory was described in the text: something warm, something from long ago, something that made you cry, something that made you laugh, and something that is as precious as gold.

Miss Lucci emphasized that the drawings did not have to be professional as long as they depicted the memory. She encouraged the students to put captions with their drawings, and then they shared their drawings with a peer. As the students shared, they added any other information they remembered about their memories.

By first drawing and talking about their memories, Miss Lucci's students began their personal narratives with specific ideas in mind. Nhat, a student who has been in the United States for two years, shares his drawings and memories below. Nhat's drawing of something from long ago, remembering his great grandma, gave him his topic for his personal narrative.

Nhat's memories: Sample drawings from the frontloading activity

1. I remember when Santa came to my house and gave me and my sister gifts; after that, I knew that my Dad's friend sent Santa to my house. I love them all.

2. I remember my great grandma died when I was in second or third grade. I feel bad because one time I hated her and hid her walking stick.

3. I remember when my family left Vietnam and flew over to America. I cried a little, but my sister cried a lot.

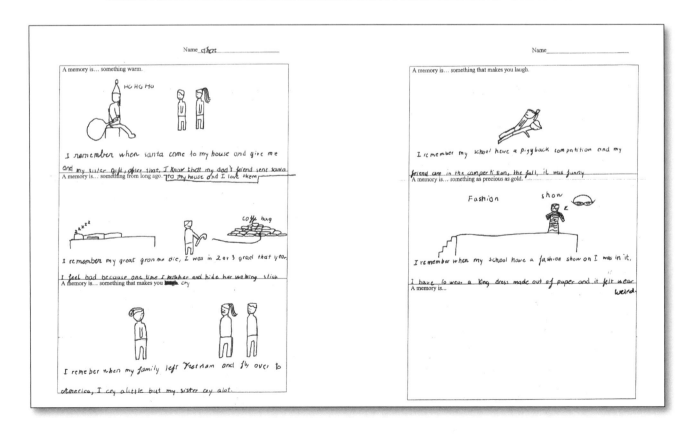

When the students had completed their first drafts, Miss Lucci explained the procedure for the *Code the Text* strategy.

Procedure

1. The students made notations with three different colored pencils in the margins of their drafts. When they found clarity, they put a *C* in the margin. When they found a descriptive detail, they put a *D* in the margin. When students found examples, they put an *E* in the margin.

2. As students saw where the C-D-E already existed in their drafts, they analyzed their work to determine whether more clarity, descriptive details, and/or examples were still needed.

3. With feedback from their teacher, peers, or parents, students revised their drafts to include additional clarity, descriptive details, and/or examples.

An Example of Student Revision

Nhat's draft

I was a kid back then (D). I usually went back to my grandparent's house every summer. I love everything in my grandparent's house but my great grandma she was around 90's (D) and old so she was a little crazy. She talked about lots of thing like "I don't want ham today" (E) but it was not even dinner yet. Sometime I was playing, then I met her, then she start to tell me what to do. I was a kid so it was kind up annoying (D). There was a night that the whole family was gathering up together and watch TV. Then I saw my great grandma walking down to the living room.

"What are you doing here? You should be in bed," my grandpa said. Then he told me to take a chair and move it to where she was standing so she can sit. I thought that she was just crazy, but as I got older, I start to have a feeling that she wanted to be with the whole family.

Teaching Tip

With Miss Lucci's guidance, Nhat decided there were eight other C-D-Es needed:

Clarity: Explain how I feel about her.

Explain back where and when.

Describe what she looks like.

Clarify how she died and describe it.

Example of how I was annoying.

Clarify grandparents who lived far away and visited every two months.

Describe grandparent's house.

Clarify "met" as in would "run into" or "see" her when I was playing and she talked to me.

Nhat's revised draft

I was a kid back then, when I was six years old and I was back in Vietnam. I usually went to my grandparents' house. Their house was beautiful. They have all kinds of trees: mangos, lemons, and coffee beans. In the morning, you could hear sound like the chirping of birds, the wind blowing against the antennae and the barking of my grandfather's dog when there was a visitor or the mailman. Their garden was so big that it's about one mile long cause they grow coffee beans. I love everything there but my great grandma.

She was around 90's and old so she was a little crazy. She can't barely walk without her walking stick. Her hair was white and Vietnam's girl's tradition cloth. She talked about lots of things like: "I don't want ham today" but it was not even dinner yet. Sometime I was playing but when I ran into her, started to tell me what to do. I was a kid so it was kinda annoying. I feel like she was lazy and trying to be the boss so I ran away.

I had lived through years with the anger within me so one day I decided to hide her walking stick. Inside my grandparent's house was a stack of coffee beans and I hid it on top of it, then went back down pretending nothing had happened. That afternoon, she can't find her walking stick so she started yelling and my mom, dad, and grandparents ran around to find it. I felt guilty so I climbed back up and took it back down. I told mom and dad everything and they feel happy that I know how to take responsibility of what I have done.

There was a night that the whole family was gathering up together and watched TV. Then I saw my great grandma walking down to the living room. "What are you doing here? You should be in bed," my grandpa said. Then he told me to take a chair and move it to where she was standing so she can sit. I thought she was crazy but as I get older, I started to have a feeling that she wanted to be with the whole family.

A few years after that, she died. I was still in school season so I could only go back there from the city and came back the next day. I feel very bad because of my foolish action and started to pray for her. Since then, I had changed what I felt about her.

2

Cut, Slash, and Burn

Focus

Many students tend to write everything down, especially when writing a personal narrative. It's what some teachers call a "get-up to go-to-bed" story. It often has ramblings and incidentals that make the writing cumbersome and even boring. When asked to condense their information, students make a conscious effort to retain what is most important in their narrative (Burke, 2003).

Frontloading Activity

For this strategy, we've used the same frontloading activity featured in the *Code the Text* strategy: It's a rich way into a personal narrative for many students.

After a reading of *Wilfrid Gordon McDonald Partridge* by Mem Fox, the students were asked to think about their memories. When the reading was completed, the students drew examples of their memories that corresponded to how a memory was described in the text: something warm, something from long ago, something that made you cry, something that made you laugh, and something that is as precious as gold.

Miss Lucci emphasized that the drawings did not have to be professional as long as they depicted the memory. She encouraged the students to put captions with their drawings, and then they shared their drawings with a peer. As the students shared, they added information they remembered about their memories.

By first drawing and then talking about their memories, Miss Lucci's students began their personal narratives with specific ideas in mind. Anna is a 15-year-old student who was born in California; most of her family is from Honduras. Her personal narrative developed from a memory she recalled from when she was 12 years old, and it was the subject of her third drawing, about something that made her laugh:

I hit my friend in the store and I ran into a pole.

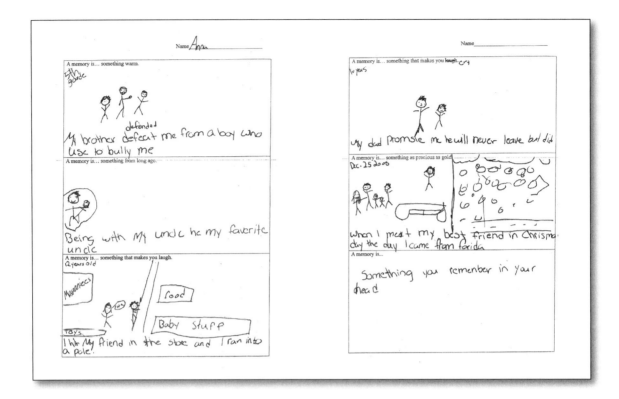

Procedure

1. The students read through their entire drafts once with intent to delete 25% of the words. (For example, a 100-word essay now becomes 75 words.) Students identify nonessential information, whether it be phrases, sentences, partial paragraphs, or whole sections. Some of these are probably the students' first thoughts and are not needed in their drafts.

2. The students may have a choice to work on this procedure independently, in pairs, or in groups of three. Some students find that their peers recognize what is essential and nonessential in the draft before they actually do.

3. While students are rewriting their drafts, remind them that, with 25% of their words gone, they may want to reorganize their ideas and add new words.

4. Students reread their drafts independently, or share their rewritten texts in pairs or groups of three.

Teaching Tip

Students who draft on the computer using Microsoft Word can check their word count after they've finished or as they're writing. They can find how to use this feature by typing "word count" into the help window at the top of the screen. Most students prefer to compose, from the beginning, directly on the computer. If they set up their programs to show the word count continuously as it changes, they will be able to revise recursively as they continue to compose.

An Example of Student Revision

Anna's draft with her deletions in bold type

One day me and my friend Cheyenne went to a grocery store. On the way to the store, she was hitting me and I couldn't hit her because she was blocking my hits. So I thought to get paybacks later. **OK, so we got there. Me and Cheyenne ran to the store. We went to the candy place then to the toy place and some other places.**

But some place that I will never forget was the amazing and book place because Me and Cheyenne was looking at mazings [magazines] and that's when the thought came back to me pay backs so I hit her really hard and I knew she was going to hit me back and I ran and I also knew that she ran fast so I turned my head to see if she was behind me in the moment I crash into a pole. And that I remember when I crash into the pole was that I can't catch air and I fell on the floor.

Cheyenne was standing there and laughing. I got up I felt dizzy but I start laughing also. Then Cheyenne started laughing even more because my neck was read all over. I got home with Cheyenne and my mom saw my neck and asked what happen. I told her and she said, "You two are just some silly girls."

This is a memory I would never forget and this is also the funniest thing that's ever happened to me.

Teaching Tip

During a conference with Miss Lucci, Anna decided that it's important to include the following:

At the magazine rack, I got my revenge.

We both started laughing, because even though I was dizzy and my neck was red, I was okay.

But she also decided it was not important to include her mom, who is not important in this story.

Anna's revised draft

One day I and my friend, Cheyenne, went to a grocery store. On the way to the store she was hitting me and I couldn't hit her because she was blocking my hits. So I thought to myself that I would get pay backs later.

At the magazine rack I got my revenge. I and Cheyenne were looking at magazines and that's when the thought came back to me . . . pay backs . . . so I hit her really hard and I knew she was going to hit me back so I ran. I also knew that she ran fast so I turn my head to see if she was behind me. In that moment I crashed into a pole. And the only thing I remember when I crashed into the pole was that I couldn't catch air and I fell on the floor.

We both started laughing because even though I was dizzy and my neck was red, I was okay. This is a memory I will never forget and this is also the funniest thing that's ever happen to me.

3

Create a
Character Sketch

Focus

A character sketch is about a fictional character, a historical character, or a person from the writer's life. An effective character sketch includes how the character thinks, feels, and behaves.

Frontloading Activity

1. Students each draw a stick figure of a character. They draw hands, a heart, and a head on their figures.

2. Students draw a line coming from the figure's **hands** and write these questions:

   What does this character do for a living?

   What does this character do for entertainment? Fun? Relaxation?

   What does this character do when angry? Upset? Happy?

   What does this character do well? What does this person struggle with?

3. Students draw a line coming from the figure's **heart** and write these questions:

   What is important to this character?

   What does this character believe in?

   What is right and wrong to this character?

   Who does this character love? What does this character love?

   Who does this character hate? What does this character hate?

4. Students draw a line coming from the figure's **head** and write these questions:

Does this character think with the brain or act on emotions?

Is this character smart? Book smart? Street smart?

What are this character's beliefs? What is important to this person?

How does this character make decisions? Who or what influences the decisions?

How does this character behave in different situations?

Procedure

1. Students should develop additional questions based upon their assignment and their character.

2. Students research, interview, and read to find the responses to the questions.

3. Students work on this procedure independently, in pairs, or in small groups to gather more information for their drafts.

4. Students revise their drafts with the additional information by organizing it according to whether it is related to the **head, heart,** or **hand.**

4

Create an Argument

Focus

When writing an argument, many students enjoy expressing their opinions, but they must realize that factual information is the heart of any argument. With the extended frontloading activity described below, the students prethink their positions to create their own arguments.

Definition

Argument: The process of developing or presenting ideas dealing with a controversial point using differing points of view.

Frontloading Activity

1. A model is read for students to analyze. Miss Lucci has used the essay below with her middle school students; it was released by the Pennsylvania Department of Education.

Student Editorial

If schools don't want to remain in the Dark Ages, they have to allow students to bring cell phones to our classes. They have become an essential part of our lives, and almost everyone has one or wants one.

If for no other reason, we need to have cell phones with us for safety. Our parents want us to have them so that if anything happens, we can get in touch with them right away. I read that my favorite teen

(Continued)

(Continued)

actress, Sara Jackson Milford, carries a cell phone to her school so that she can call her home or her agent whenever she wants. My mom says that she has more peace of mind because she knows that I can call her whenever I need her. Parents call us on cell phones for little everyday things, too, like reminding us of a dental appointment or a piano lesson, or telling us about a change in plans. Without our cell phones, they would have to call and bother someone in the school office to get a message to us. Or we just wouldn't know and would miss the appointment or lesson, or find out about a change in plans after riding the bus home instead of waiting to be picked up at school. Cell phones simplify things for everyone.

Cell phones that can take pictures are helpful, too. You can use them for class, for photo essays and things like that. They are even being used to help solve crimes. In Australia, neighborhood watch groups are using cell phones in policing their communities. In Japan, people can send pictures directly to the police. Having cell phones in school could help cut down on vandalism or other inappropriate behavior as any student could click a picture of the culprit and share it with the principal or the authorities.

The students at one high school in Florida helped to convince state legislators to change the law that banned cell phones in schools. Now individual school districts set their own policies. At this Florida high school, students can have cell phones at school, but they have to be turned off and kept in their lockers. Still, they get to have them there so that they can use them as soon as school is out. The principal said that most of the 1,700 students there have cell phones.

There's no point in sticking our heads in the sand. The world is changing quickly, and our school policies need to change to keep up with them. Cell phones are just a fact of life. They aren't going away.

Source: Grade 7, Reading Item Sampler 2008–2009, The Pennsylvania System of School Assessment.

2. A discussion of the essay revolves around the following questions:
   - Does the writer know the audience? Why or why not?
   - What is the writer's point of view of the argument?
   - What details support the action the writer wants the audience to take?
   - Which facts support the action the writer wants the audience to take?
   - How does the writer's research affect the draft?
   - Does the writer provide a strong argument to support her stance?
   - Does the writer anticipate the audience's acceptance of her explanation or evaluation of the concept or problem in the argument?

Teaching Tip

Depending on the reading and writing level of the students, the students may find it helpful if the answers generated to the questions above are recorded on a white board for them to see.

3. Following the discussion, the students continue the frontloading activity through role-playing. This helps the students to think about the different perspectives that will be addressed in their arguments. Ample facts and details are needed to sway the audience to accept the writer's point of view. Three students discuss the use of cell phones through role-playing prior to writing their own arguments. The students play the roles of the teacher (T), the principal (P), and the student (S). Their interaction might look something like this:

T- I think that cell phones should not belong in school, because it will create a distraction in school, plus there would be less learning and more texting.

P- I think students should have cell phones, because fewer kids would skip school, and kids would like school better.

T- Kids come to school regardless of whether they have a phone or not.

S- I think we should have cell phones, because most cell phones have calculators.

P- Saves money, since students don't have to buy a separate calculator.

T- How do students use the calculator if they are texting?

S- Some phones multitask.

P- Yeah, but it takes five seconds to write a text message.

S- If we had cell phones, I would be on Facebook.

T- See, cell phones can be a distraction.

P- Cell phones can be both helpful and distracting.

Procedure

1. While rereading their drafts, the students use a colored pencil to identify any information, at any point in the draft, that expresses their point of view.

2. Next, the students use a pencil of a different color to underline the details that support the action the writer wants the audience to take.

3. A third color is used to underline the facts that support the action the writer wants the audience to take.

4. A fourth color is used to underline any information that helps the audience to accept the author's explanation or evaluation of the concept or problem. This could include any facts or details that have already been identified.

5. Students analyze their drafts using the colored underlined areas as an indication of what is already there, what information may still be needed, and whether any information needs to be deleted. Before rewriting, the students may need to research to find more information to support their arguments.

6. The students revise their drafts, incorporating any new details that may support their arguments. This may include both facts and details to help the audience accept their positions.

7. The students share their revised drafts with their peers, teachers, or parents.

An Example of Student Revision

Daniel's introductory paragraph

First, we need to save the environment before it's too late. We can do this by finding substitutes for fuels we use today. Second, buy products that are safer for the earth. Third, take care of the earth. That's have a better planet and save it so we don't have to live in a trash filled earth.

During a conference, Daniel and his teacher discussed the following questions: What is the main idea of the essay? What details support the main idea? Which facts support the author's position? How does the author's opinion affect the draft? Does the author provide a strong argument to support his stance? Daniel realized he didn't have his main idea clearly stated, and he needed to add details to his essay.

Daniel's revised introductory paragraph

Imagine stepping out of your front door into a trash filled yard, breathing in smog and gasoline. You couldn't breathe. This is how our Earth will be if we don't save it. First, we need to save the environment before it's too late. We can do this by finding substitutes for fuels we use today. Second, we should buy products that are safer for the earth. Third, take care of the earth. Then we'll have a better planet so we don't have to live in a trash filled earth.

5

Write an Effective Speech

Focus

When students write speeches, they need to think about the impact that the human voice brings to the written word. Before a speech can be well delivered, it has to be well written.

Frontloading Activity

1. The teacher shares speeches that are relevant to the content that the students are studying as a frontloading activity. Many speeches are readily available on the Internet. For example,

   - If the students are learning about World War II, some excellent speeches include Franklin Roosevelt's "Day of Infamy" given on December 7, 1941, and Winston Churchill's "We Shall Fight Them on the Beaches," given on June 4, 1940.
   - If the students are learning about the civil rights movement, Martin Luther King's "I Have a Dream" speech from August 28, 1963, would be appropriate.

2. The teacher and students analyze and discuss what made these speeches famous.

   - How does the speech open?
   - How is the content conveyed in the body of the speech?
   - How many points are covered?
   - Are rhetorical questions included?
   - Is there humor or an anecdote to explain a point?
   - Is there a strong concluding statement?

3. Then the students write their own speeches after analyzing the models. Depending on the class and the assignment, the students focus either on a specific time period that they are studying or on specific content they are learning.

Procedure

1. Students read their speech drafts aloud for a peer, teacher, or parent. They practice their speeches with attentiveness to sentence fluency and voice.

2. Then they revise their speeches with the feedback they received from their peers, teacher, or parents. Students use the following questions as a guide (but not all questions need to be answered in one speech):

   - In the introduction, is there a thoughtful question?
     - Is there a dramatic story or funny anecdote?
     - Is there a meaningful quotation?
     - Is there a strong statement about the topic?
   - In the body, did I arrange the information correctly?
     - Are there sufficient facts and details?
     - Are there clear descriptions and explanations?
     - Are opinions supported with logical reasons and solid facts?
   - In the conclusion, is there a relevant story or eye-opening fact?
     - Is emphasis placed on the importance of the topic?
     - Are the most important ideas summarized?

3. Their revised speeches are shared with a peer, teacher, or parent before they are performed.

4. The emphasis shifts from the written word to the spoken word. After practice and further feedback, the speeches are ready for delivery to an audience.

Teaching Tip

The following website gives valuable information on how to deliver effective speeches: www.ehow .com/how-to_4845368_5_deliver-effective-speeches.html.

PART II

Focus on Ideas

Words on Writing From Gordon Korman

I tend to overwrite my first drafts, so revision is more than just separating the wheat from the chaff. Often, that's where I discover what my story is really about. Also, the rewriting process is where the novel gets its pacing and momentum—which is especially important for reluctant readers.

Ideas are the heart of any text. Readers read for ideas, whether they are presented as information, opinions, or stories. In order to communicate their ideas, students need to be mindful of the purpose and audience of their writing as well as be knowledgeable about their topic. Ideas can be developed and woven into writing in many forms: within a "story" as in the revision strategy *Use an Anecdote*; within the details of a piece, as demonstrated in *Search for Details, Guided Reading,* and *Reread and Rewrite*; or even within the sensory description that elaborates a personal story, as in the *Expand a Memory/Expand the Text* strategy. Focusing on ideas moves students in the **Write direction** by encouraging them to revise the details that will help to convey their ideas.

The Revision Strategies in Part II Correlated to the 6 Traits of Effective Writing

Strategy/6 Traits	Ideas	Organization	Voice	Word Choice	Sentence Fluency
Use Anecdotes	•		•		
Expand a Memory	•	•			
Guided Revising	•			•	
Search for Details	•				
Reread and Rewrite	•	•	•		
Add Specifics	•				

Note: Since the revision strategies do not address Conventions, this trait is not represented in this chart.

6

Use Anecdotes

Focus

Sometimes students come to a stand-still in their writing—they are at a loss for ideas or unsure of which direction to take next. Learning to use an anecdote as an idea-generator can help students expand and illustrate writing and, most important of all, give them a feeling of personal involvement and excitement that allows them to be creative. In this strategy, students add anecdotes to their writing to enhance the content and the style of the piece. It is a revision technique that gives high school students a chance to use narrative skills in their expository writing. It is also a way for them to find and exercise their unique individual voices, a quality often lacking in students' expository writing.

Teaching Tip

The teacher reviews the concept of anecdote with the class and stresses the following explanation of anecdotes:

The anecdote is a short account of a particular incident or event of an interesting or amusing nature, a brief story used to illustrate a point that often includes dialogue and almost always features characters.

Procedure

1. One method of modeling is to find a generic or bland piece of writing to use as an example and then identify a place within it to insert an anecdote.

   • Find a news magazine or newspaper article and make a copy of the article to project for discussion.
   • Insert small anecdotes into the model articles to show students how effective this makes the writing. Or, if the article begins with an anecdote, discuss its effect.

2. After the modeling session, guide students back to their own writing to think about areas where an anecdote is appropriate.

3. Have the students find at least one place where they could expand or illustrate a point by using an anecdote.

4. Have them pinpoint a place in their drafts where an anecdote would bring more information. Writing an anecdote makes a deeper point than adding a one- or two-word detail.

5. Encourage students to be creative and use their narrative skills. They can write an anecdote from their own lives, which will make their writing authentic, or they can research to find an anecdote that will fit nearly any situation in writing.

Teaching Tip

One method of using an anecdote is to begin the anecdote in the introduction, and return to it and finish it or comment on it in the conclusion. Students write the anecdote, explain a concept introduced in the anecdote, and then return to it in the end. This strengthens the organization, content, and voice of the draft.

When writing for high school and content areas, students are encouraged to use facts and opinions presented by authorities. Students frequently craft tight, interesting anecdotes that nicely illustrate explanatory/informational writing to expand the main idea.

An Example of Student Revision

Stephanie's original fourth paragraph

On another day my family and I went to swim with dolphins. The dolphins were in a giant pool and each person was allowed to swim with them for a few minutes.

After self critiquing and peer- and teacher-conferencing, Stephanie's elaborated and revised paragraphs with an anecdote

On another day my family and I went to swim with dolphins. I was ten years old. The pool was terrifically big. One could fit a blimp in there. After a temporary wait, I had my chance to ride the dolphin. I had been watching the dolphins and one seemed particularly aggressive. This was the dolphin the trainer gave me to ride.

The terror built within me. How could I ride such a menacing dolphin? I caught the dolphin's eye and he seemed to glare at me. All through this, the trainer was laughing and smiling. I could tell he was in on the plot.

As my quivering hands held on to the slippery fin, the dolphin began to swim. He accelerated faster and faster until I thought he was moving at warp speed. Then the unthinkable happened. The dolphin roared up on his caudal fin and twisted hard to the right. My life flashed before my eyes and it felt like the feeling of falling back in a chair. Time slowed. I could count every single heartbeat. The dolphin went back down. Time started to flow. My heart slowed. As the dolphin began to return to the dock, I realized that my fear had been for naught. It dawned on me that this dolphin was not trying to hurt me, that it was a friendly beast, that it really just wanted another fish from the trainer. Thus, my experience with the dolphin came to a rather surprisingly pleasant close.

7

Expand the Memory, Expand the Text

Focus

Students often write a piece from memory, and it will be "true" to what happened but surprisingly free of details and ideas. This expansion strategy works well to have students revisit a memory and a text to improve the writing. Barry Lane developed this strategy to help students expand on ideas that are already included in their writing. "Explode a Moment" (Lane, 2008) encourages writers to take a small detail and explode it into something bigger, and explosions are always interesting! Encouraging writers to ask themselves questions about what they are writing, then answer those questions, produces more detailed and vivid writing. As students think about the many possible descriptors such as colors, sounds, touch, smell, texture, and even the weather, they expand the details in their writing with these points of interest. As a result, their memory pieces suddenly become more vivid and alive with improved imagery.

Procedure

1. The teacher generates a freewriting to model the strategy. Freewriting is writing continuously while putting thoughts into words, phrases, or sentences without pausing to think deeply about them. The freewriting process can range from seconds to minutes as its primary purpose is to foster fluency in the writer and the text.

2. Have students think of a memory that lasted a few seconds but was important to them. Encourage them to think of this vivid moment—something that they remember. It can be from home, from school, and from any age.

3. Guide students into freewriting for 15 minutes about that memory. Have them try to fill at least one page.
   - Remind them that each detail they come up with makes that memory more real and vivid for the reader.
   - If they get stuck, as students often do with freewriting, have them think of questions to help add details:
     - What smells did I sense?
     - What color was it?
     - Where did it happen?
   - Sensory questions tend to help students expand their texts when they are freewriting.

4. Remind students they are writing about one memory and they should not go on to the next day or next point.

5. At the end of 15 minutes, have students stop and read over their texts.

6. Have students circle a detail in what they have written; it can be a favorite detail; one that makes them angry, nostalgic, or happy; or just a detail that stands out and is memorable to them.

7. At the bottom of the page, they are to add three to five more details.

8. In revision groups or on their own, have students read the pieces again, make observations about what they have written, and ask questions again of the text.
   - What color was it?
   - Why is this detail so special to you/me?
   - Was anyone else there?
   - What smells could you sense?
   - Were there any noises you/I remember? and so forth.

9. Now, students are armed with more details and ideas to expand their text.

With these questions and observations fresh in their minds, students can add the details from the bottom of the page, or details that arose from the questions and observations in their revision groups to their freewriting. They could also make the questions into the lead of the piece. This is the heart of "expanding the memory." Upon probing a text, many more details will come to mind as they remember more of the "moment." Often, these are details and ideas they did not have in their mind when they wrote the piece, but that can now be used to expand the text.

Teaching Tip

As an extension, students could take one of the questions, turn it into a lead, and then produce another freewriting from that lead for another 10 to 15 minutes, expanding that moment.

When finished, students will have a freewriting that is more focused through the addition of details. This *Expand the Memory/Expand the Text* writing can easily be included in the draft of another text.

8

Guided Revising

Focus

The late Donald Graves, a master teacher of writing, was a strong proponent of revision. He and his colleague Penny Kittle penned a book (2005) about writing in which they called attention to the importance of rereading text and revising, and this strategy comes from that work. As teachers realize, students need to reread their work frequently, because what they *think* they wrote is not always what they *actually* wrote. However, the process of rereading and rethinking takes guidance, not merely a direction to "Read it over and look for areas to revise."

This strategy guides writers through specific parts of their works, such as a favorite sentence, an inspired word grouping, or a section that speaks to the "heartbeat" (HB) of the piece. Once these effective parts of a piece are identified, students study how they have used detail, style, and voice to achieve them, concentrating on how each part works.

By reading for specifics, students have a plan of what to look for and what they may need to change, and they can learn how to make good drafts even better. Using this strategy that encourages deeper inspection of their work, students attend to the overall meaning of the writing and are given the tools they need to improve presentation of ideas, sentence fluency, and voice.

Procedure

1. Have the students do a first reading of their drafts. As they do this, guide them to look for the following:

   - Find a sentence you really like—underline it.
   - Find three words you really like—circle them.
   - Find a paragraph or section that "surprises" you. Put slash marks at the beginning and end of it.

2. Once the first reading is complete, guide the students into a second reading, this time looking for what Graves and Kittle (2005) call the "Heartbeat," or the central idea of their drafts. Help students as they complete the following:

   - Look for a sentence that contains the HB, the main point of what they want to say, and mark it with "HB."
   - Next, look for phrases or sentences that clarify the HB. Put brackets around them—they can be in separate places throughout the piece; they also can be partial sentences.
   - After these are identified and marked, look for two or more sentences that have little to do with the story or the subject. Mark these with question marks.

3. Then have students read their drafts aloud—or have peers read each others' drafts aloud—and find or listen for four words they like the sound of, circling them in red.

4. Now it is time for a third rereading. Guide the students to focus on words and sentences that are vivid and precise, asking them to

   - look for three verbs that are precise and vivid, and circle them in green.
   - look for a sentence that is simple and direct and contains no clauses. Mark it with "SS."
   - look for three nouns that represent additional information they have included or could include:
     o An example is a tackle box—what items are in a tackle box?
     o Another example is a sewing bag—what items are in a sewing bag?

5. Bring closure. When the procedure is finished, review the text and the marks, keeping in mind the new ideas and the new ways of revising the draft that have surfaced. This review can be done by looking back at the marks with the student, or by having students work with peers, commenting on the marks and discovering through collaboration how to strengthen the piece.

Teaching Tip

By implementing this guided strategy of close reading and rereading, students examine the words, phrases, and sentences that support the central idea. The students discover if their central themes need to be expanded. This strategy also shows students areas where they may have included phrases, sentences, or information that has nothing to do with the central idea.

This strategy works well for students who are concentrating on informational and persuasive writing. The advanced rereading helps to tighten and clarify writing and may eliminate problems that could surface during the editing stage.

An Example of Student Revision

Kiki's original draft with annotations in parentheses and featured words in bold

Dear Mr. Webster,

I think Harlan Rowe should have a student lounge (**HB and SS**). The teachers have one, and we **work** (circled verb) just as hard as them. As students, we do worksheets, projects, tests, **quizzes** (like the sound), and other work all throughout the day. By **midday** (word I really like) we are very tired out, which is why a student lounge would be a perfect place to relax.

/You may not **realize** (circled verb) it, but students do have a lot of extra time during the day./ Students can **visit** (like the sound) the lounge in-between classes, during study halls, or when they're done eating at lunch. Also, teachers can **send** (like the sound) us there when we're done with what we are doing in class.

The lounge could have furniture and snacks (noun with additional information). There could be couches and all kinds of **comfortable** (word I really like) chairs. [Also, we could have drink and vending machines]. **All the money made from the machines could go toward more things for the lounge** (noun with additional information). [We could also do **fundraisers** (word I really like) like dances, carwashes, and selling things]. Now, I know what you're thinking, kids will go crazy in a fun room. **I agree we should have a teacher in there at all times** (SS).

As you can see, [I have everything planned out for a new student lounge]. Students can go many different times during the day. [We can have furniture, snacks, and drinks]. We can [pay for everything through fundraisers] and there can be a teacher there at all times. [So, you should strongly **consider** (circled verb) adding a student lounge at our school, Harlan Rowe].

Sincerely (like the sound),
Kiki

9

Hunt for Details

Focus

Effective writing has depth and details. When students revise for clarity of ideas in their drafts, it is best to break this complicated thinking skill into smaller chunks—and one of those is how to revise for details. When students identify the types of details they've used, it helps them to see if their writing has enough depth. The teacher should first explain what "details" are and, using a student's paper as a model, show the students how to identify them.

Procedure

1. Students read their drafts, and using a different color ink or colored pencil, circle all details. These circles will make the number of details, or lack thereof, visually apparent.

2. Below is a list of the types of details found in many genres of writing. Teachers can collaborate with their students and make a list of the types of details found in the specific writing they are revising. In addition to circling the details, students should write, next to each circled detail, what type of detail it is.

   - Facts
   - Numbers and statistics
   - Authoritative opinions
   - Descriptions
   - Procedures
   - Events
   - Sensory details
   - People, places, and ideas
   - Dates
   - Measurements
   - Anecdotes

3. Caution the students that the goal is not to pack their drafts with inappropriate details. The object is high-quality, appropriate information, not just a list of details.

4. After identifying the details, the students then decide what **details are missing**, what **details do not enhance** the writing, and if the **placement of the details best supports** the topic or subject of the writing.

Teaching Tip

To help students understand the thinking and the process of revision, collect their first drafts before they revise. Read their drafts without making any marks on them, but write two to three thoughtful questions at the conclusion of each draft. Use the five *W*s and an *H* as your guide: Who? Where? Why? When? What? and How? Ask students to elaborate on a topic, incident, or event. Guiding them with questions will help them think through their writing.

10

Reread and Rewrite

Focus

Many students, upon finishing a draft, believe the text is surely finished. Without training and guidance to revisit the text, they may submit what they think is finished, only to later discover there are gaps in the thinking and the text. With this strategy, students try to free their minds from the text in front of them to improve the ideas and the organization. By drawing on a free-thinking approach, students can consider their texts and discover different means of improving the work. Ideas and organization are the main focus with this strategy.

Procedure

Reread

1. The students read the text. This can be a piece from their writer's notebook, a free-write, or a rough draft.

2. After reading, they go back and circle, underline, or highlight whole sections that make sense, that have details, or that they find interesting. Whether these sections are phrases, sentences, partial paragraphs, or whole sections, they are so obvious they glow.

3. After identifying these strong sections, students should copy them in a variety of ways:

   - Try typing them.
   - Try writing them on paper.
   - Try extending them onto another piece of paper.

4. Then students should use these strong words, phrases, or sentences as jumping off points for extending the text or writing new text.

5. Students should use their strong passages verbatim: "Don't change words, because in this practice you are deepening your ability to trust your own voice" (Goldberg, 1986).

Rewrite

1. The students choose a piece of writing—this could be a freewrite (a continuous writing of thoughts into words, phrases, or sentences without pausing to think deeply about it) or a draft for any project. (Note: This works best if there is a day or two between the first writing and the reading. Give the students time to reread the writing carefully.)

2. Using the method of "timed writing"—choosing a time and rewriting the passage within that block of time—students rewrite the passage.

3. After giving the writing a rest for another day; students rewrite the passage again.

4. And again, another day. With each rewriting, new ways of seeing the topic emerge, new structures of sentences come forth, and new details are added to the page.

5. When students have completed several of these rewrites, it is time to take all the versions of the piece and pull them together.

11

Add Specifics

Focus

There are times when students have little idea where to begin revising. They can read and read over their texts and still not have a clear idea of where to begin and what to do. This strategy gives them a starting place. It is a random starting place, but a starting place, nonetheless. In this strategy, the writer or a peer "points" to a random spot in the text; the spot is then labeled, and the writer begins to add narrative or detail.

Three more variations of this strategy lead the student to add colors, sounds, and metaphors, or to identify when weak adjectives have been used. Thus students begin to add specific words, phrases, and sentences as they clarify their thoughts. They will be using a mixture of conventions and concepts to carry out this strategy: combining grammar and syntax with figurative language. Students will soon be pointing at all sorts of things! Better yet, they will be revising.

Procedure

There are many possible variations of this strategy. For three of the four described here, the students can identify the passage to be revised in either of two ways:

1. Students take a text, close their eyes, and point their finger onto the page. Wherever it lands is the starting point for revision.

2. Students take a text, read it carefully, and determine where they want to begin the revision detailed below. (This is necessary for Variation #3.)

Variation #1

At the end of the sentence or the paragraph nearest where the finger lands, the student writes, "**For example,**" and then adds a narrative or detail to back up the point of that sentence or that paragraph. The narrative can be an anecdote; it could be a sensory detail; it could be a specific detail; it could be a series of details. Whatever the choice, it needs to be a detail that will clarify the sentence immediately before it.

Variation #2

Students read through the text carefully and add **colors, sounds,** and **metaphors** in a minimum of **three** places.

Variation #3

1. Students read through the text looking for the following words: **nice, big, good, bad, old,** and **young.**

2. Students circle those weak adjectives.

3. Students replace each of the weak adjectives with a **complete sentence** that is more specific and exact in describing the thing that the weak adjective modified.

Variation #4

If the piece is a poem or a narrative, or even an informational piece or a persuasive piece with a character, students can try adding a memory, a dream, a flashback, or a description of the character.

An Example of Student Revision

Maggie's revised second paragraph of her persuasive essay, with the added text in bold

Out of the hundreds of reasons that could support keeping the school week as it is, the energy of the students stands out the most. Already, students are staying up at night way too late, just to do their homework. Adding hours to the school day will just make it worse. **Dinner-times would be pushed back, leaving less time for homework.** Teachers, take in mind that students will probably be falling asleep in your classes because of this. Nowadays it seems like too many students are exhausted by 3:20 as it is. Elongating the day will result in students sleeping through class or just not getting enough sleep.

PART III

Focus on Organization

Words on Writing From Sara Holbrook

You wouldn't know it to look at my spice cabinet or laundry room, but I am very organized in my writing. In prose, I work from an outline, often hand written with arrows and bubbles and numbered sequences. In writing poetry I like to sneeze a lot of related, observational words on the page and then revise by reordering them, moving them around like Legos until they snap together right. As soon as I have a first draft I take a deep breath and (in my mind) go back to begin to fix my first pass at the writing. Knowing that revision is coming is very freeing for me because I know I don't have to get it right the first time. If it weren't for the opportunity of revision, I would be frozen in place when facing the blank page.

The way information is presented to the reader has an enormous impact on the effectiveness of any piece of writing. Revising for organization strengthens a draft by improving the fluency of the content. The revision strategies *ABC, Tally Up,* and *Snip 'n' Clip* encourage students to think about how they organize their sentences, how to combine and reorder their sentences, and how to vary their sentence beginnings. The strategy *Organize a Feature Article* helps students organize their findings and interviews to create a cohesive article for a newspaper or magazine. *Try a Different Genre* takes a more radical approach; with this strategy, students are challenged to revise their writing by altering the starting genre of their draft: changing a narrative text to a poem, for example, or an email to an expository text, or a letter to an essay. Stepping outside the boundaries of the original genre helps students to focus on the essential ideas in the text and the most effective way to present them.

The Revision Strategies in Part III Correlated to the 6 Traits of Effective Writing

Strategy/6 Traits	Ideas	Organization	Voice	Word Choice	Sentence Fluency
ABC Revision	•	•		•	•
Feature Article	•	•			
Try a Different Genre	•	•	•		
Snip 'n' Clip		•			•
Tally Up		•			•

Note: Since the revision strategies do not address Conventions, this trait is not represented in this chart.

12

ABC Revision

Focus

Often, when students begin to write a piece, the sentences in their drafts are very similar to one another, with little variety in structure. The result is stilted, repetitive writing. Using the ABC strategy, an exercise in style and imagination, is sure to help those writers who get stuck with too many sentences that start with the same word or that follow the same pattern of length and construction. Students become more thoughtful and creative as they search for ways to rewrite sentences constrained by one rule: The first letter of each sentence must be in alphabetical order. This game-like strategy never feels like drudgery and is a great way to add diversity to writing.

Procedure

1. Students choose a draft and read it aloud. As they read, they pay attention to the beginnings of the sentences and how these beginnings sound. When students read a piece aloud, the cadence of the writing will become more apparent than in a silent reading.

2. Students then rewrite the draft or a part of the draft, beginning with the first sentence of the selected text.

3. The rewrite follows the following format (hence, the term *ABC Revision*):

   • The first word in the first sentence begins with the letter *A*.
   • The first word in the second sentence begins with the letter *B*.
   • Subsequent sentences start with subsequent letters in alphabetical order.

4. Students write until they have finished rewriting all sentences of the selected text, using all or some of the alphabet. (If some students balk at the difficulty imposed by this format, allow them sentences between the alphabet letters—call them interrupter sentences).

Variations

1. If the draft is brief, students can begin anywhere in the alphabet and continue rewriting sentences until they have completed rewriting the text (whether or not they have used up the whole alphabet). It is not necessary to use all the letters to create effective variety in sentence beginnings and structure. Using 22 letters works fine, because that allows students to leave out 4 difficult letters. Many students like this technique and take it as a challenge.

2. Another twist on this strategy is to let students choose a word or phrase, maybe their names, the school mascot, or any configuration of letters they like. Then, instead of rewriting to fit the alphabet, the letters of the chosen word are worked into the draft as initial letters of the first word in each sentence. Maybe someone will use the title of the work. There is no end to the creativity that is possible.

An Example of Student Revision

Courtney's draft

The School Day

> Hi, my name is Courtney G. . . and I am going to describe a normal day at school for me. The first thing that happens is the bell rings at 8:00 a.m. You will either wait outside for the bell to ring, or if it's cold out, the teachers will let you wait in the gym. At 8:22, classes start after an 18 minute homeroom. In homeroom the teachers take roll and we listen to the announcements. Morning advisory is the same every day. The first period starts at 8:22 a.m. and for me that's fun period. Having good grades in these classes is just as important and hard as regular classes. These classes are a lot of fun though; there's Tech Ed, Family Consumer Science, music class, and of course art. The first marking period you'll have one of these, then the next marking period you'll have a different one, and so on.

Courtney's revised draft

The School Day

> **As** the bell rings at 8:00 a.m. the school day starts and students fill the halls. **Being** a student you will either wait outside for the bell to ring, or if it's cold out, the teachers will let you wait in the gym. **Classes** will start at 8:22 a.m., but before that you spend 18 minutes in A.M. Homeroom which we call advisory. **During** homeroom the teachers take roll, and we listen to the announcements over the loudspeakers. **Every** day morning advisory is the same, and I'll tell you about P.M. Advisory later. **First** period starts at 8:22 and for me that's fun period, but don't be fooled by the name. **Getting** good grades in these classes are just as important and hard as regular classes. **Having** these classes is a lot of fun though, there's Tech Ed (wood shop), Family Consumer Science, music class, and of course art. **In** the first marking period, you'll have one of these, then the next marking period you'll have a different one, and so on.

13

Feature Article

Focus

Writing a feature article about a person may be a daunting task for some students. First, they have to interview their subjects, and then they have to gather additional information through research. Finally, they need to organize all of the information into a meaningful article. We have found that our middle school and junior high students accomplish this task best when they are given a set of directives to guide them through the process.

Procedure

1. The students read through the information that they have gathered through interviewing individuals and researching the individuals' pasts; often, rich material can be gathered by interviewing elders in the community. Some students keep this information in composition notebooks.

2. Then they use highlighters to organize the information for each section of their feature articles using a color scheme; an example is shown in the table below:

Sections of the Article	Highlighted Color
Biographical information	yellow
Family information	green
Person's qualities/characteristics	blue
Impact made by the person	pink

3. The students usually begin working in pairs, helping each other make decisions as to where the information should be placed.

4. Often, the highlighted information for one section of the piece will be scattered throughout the students' notes; for example, biographical information highlighted in yellow may be in different places on several different pages. The highlighting helps students visually organize the information and see if more information is needed for any of the sections.

5. The students then independently arrange their ideas and their research to write their feature articles, using the highlighting as an organizational tool.

6. Next, the students read their drafts independently or share them with a peer, a teacher, or a parent. The focus is threefold:

   - Is the information in the proper section?
   - Does each section of the article have sufficient information?
   - Is the draft free of any unnecessarily repeated information?

   If the answer to any of these questions is "no," students rearrange their drafts.

7. Finally, students highlight their articles with their colored markers one more time. This time the color should be consistent within each paragraph. They love to see how all of their information has become organized into their feature articles.

Teaching Tip

In many middle school integrated curriculums and high school graduation projects, the feature article is one integral part of an oral history project where students interview, research, photograph, and write about a person whose stories guide them into learning about the past (Dickson, Heyler, Reilly, & Romano, 2006).

All of the 180 eighth-grade students in Athens Area School District do the oral history project as a yearlong project; the example of student writing that follows came from this initiative. Teachers guide their students through the process in weekly sessions throughout the fall, and the writing portion of the project becomes intense during January and February. The culmination of the project is an oral history fair in the spring; over 1,200 people come to learn about people's stories and the past.

An Example of Student Revision

Maria has interviewed and written about her grandmother. The interview questions were printed from the oral history project book and pasted in a composition notebook to keep the information organized. After collecting all the information, Maria wrote her first draft. After highlighting, Maria realized she had missed some important information. She had to add two additional paragraphs between the third and fourth paragraphs. Her fifth paragraph became her fifth and sixth paragraphs with additional information.

Maria's original paragraph

Growing up in Scranton, Ruth went to the Patrick Henry #23 School, which ran from first to sixth grade. It was a very old school which housed two grades per classroom, and the first and second grade room was a two-seat class (two kids per desk). There were about 15 kids per class with only one teacher. Ruth and her siblings always walked to and from school. Once the school day was over though, it was time to play. Ruth liked games such as jump rope, four-square, Monopoly, and playing with dolls.

Maria's revised fifth and sixth paragraphs

Growing up in Scranton, Ruth went to the Patrick Henry #23 School, which ran from first to sixth grade. It was a very old school which housed two grades per classroom, and the first and second grade room was a two-seat class (two kids per desk). There were about 15 kids per class with one teacher.

Ruth and her siblings always walked to and from school. Once the school day was over, though, it was time to play (after chores, of course). Ruth liked games such as jump rope, four-square, Monopoly, and playing with dolls. However, this was during the Great Depression, and sometimes these things could be scarce (Later, during World War II, this became even more true, as most materials were being used in the war effort). Her family never feared for lack of food though. "My father always said, 'The Lord will provide' and He always did," said Ruth. So even though this was during the Great Depression, this was a relatively happy and peaceful time for the family.

14

Try a Different Genre

Focus

Sometimes students will finish a draft, or several stages of a draft, and then find they cannot break their "train of thought." They look at the basic words, sentences, and structure of the draft as they read over it without gaining a sense of how the piece might be read by someone else.

This strategy is designed to help students examine their thoughts and write "through different lenses." By employing *Try a Different Genre*, students can create a new draft, experiment with different structures, and play with language, ideas, and form. Here students revise their writing by crafting their original drafts into a new genre. This fundamental rethinking strategy enables students to revise by using the organization, word choice, voice, and sentence fluency of another genre to present their ideas.

Procedure

1. Students brainstorm a list of genres, which could include poems, plays, song lyrics, e-mails, text messages, blogs, short stories, letters, journals, personal essays, articles, memoirs, interviews, notes, instructional manuals, and magazine and newspaper articles.

2. The teacher models the strategy by taking an existing draft and transforming it from one genre into another. For example, an essay can be crafted into a poem or book review; science lab notes can be developed into a poem or a journal entry; a business letter can be developed into an e-mail message. This entails following the *SMART* format as much as possible:

   - Substitute information and details
   - Move words, sentences, textual material
   - Add details and information
   - Remove information
   - Think

3. The teacher should stress that the draft is not merely being rewritten. It is too easy to rewrite an essay as a letter or a poem by putting the existing sentences into a different form. While this might work, it doesn't allow the student to rethink and re-see the work in a new way.

4. Students reread their original drafts and select a draft and an appropriate genre.

5. Students craft their new drafts using the new genre.

6. Students share their new drafts with their peers.

7. Students rethink the structure, organization, and ideas of their new drafts to add information, depending on the selected genre.

8. Students determine the voice to be used in the genre they selected

Variation

Once students have selected their first draft to rework, the teacher may direct them to do a practice reworking by giving them a choice of two genres—poem and a journal entry are what most students are immediately familiar with. After they redevelop the draft into one of these two genres, students select a genre from the brainstorm list for their next reworking. After alternate genres have been explored, it is time to rework the new thoughts into a new draft in the original genre. For example, an essay is reworked to a poem and then reworked to a series of text messages, and then the original essay is rewritten. When finished with the final reworking of the draft after exploring different genres, students decide which piece is to become their final draft to be placed into their portfolios.

Teaching Tip

The best form of peer conferencing for this strategy is partners. There is much rethinking and working here, and the work can become unwieldy for a small group. Work between two partners is ideal. Read, exchange, read to each other, and rework the draft.

An Example of Student Revision

Kiki's original draft

To begin with, IHOP is a great family restaurant. There is amazing breakfast for kids such as the funny face pancakes served with whipped cream and M and M's. Though that is only the beginning at IHOP. There are also chocolate chip, strawberry, blueberry, cherry, almond, pecan, and of course plain. IHOP has a great family atmosphere and friendly employees.

Furthermore, IHOP is a great change of pace from most of the restaurants around here. In Athens, we have over four Italian restaurants and at least three Chinese buffets. Also, we have Burger King,

McDonalds, and Wendy's. So if you live in Athens and want a meal your only choices are Chinese, Italian, or fast food. IHOP offers quality food that is different than anything else in Athens.

Another reason to have an IHOP here is, it opens up new jobs in the community. In Athens, there are a lot of people who have recently lost their jobs. An IHOP would need chefs, waiters/waitress, managers, and many other employees. Also, an IHOP could sponsor local sports teams like soccer, baseball, or football.

Kiki's revised draft redeveloped from narrative to poem

As I enter through the doors, all I can see in every direction,

Is families together, it's simple perfection.

The excitement that every child's expression makes,

As they stare down at their funny face pancakes.

A mountain of M and M's and whipped cream,

You can tell this is the breakfast of their dreams.

However, if the funny face pancake isn't your kind,

There are many other options you will find.

Need a break from Italian or Chinese?

With an IHOP you'll be pleased.

After eating here it will seem rude,

To even consider fast food.

If you have just been fired there is no need to sob,

Here at IHOP you may find a job.

Waiters and waitresses have their perks,

But there are many other options for your work.

Although, some of our profits do not stay,

We give them to local sports teams so they can play.

15

Snip 'n' Clip

Focus

Some students need to physically take apart what they have written in order to make revisions to their original drafts. Once they have snipped their sentences apart, they are free to rearrange and add information where they feel it is needed. Linda Hoyt (2000) has encouraged writers in Grades K–5 to "revise with scissors," but we have found this strategy also works with some middle and high school students as well. The *Snip 'n Clip* strategy is especially useful for visual learners and those who prefer tactile experiences.

Teaching Tip

As students begin to write their drafts, direct them to write on every other line, skipping a line in between as they write. Also tell them to write on only the front side of the paper. This makes it easier for them to snip. Students will need their drafts, scissors, blank paper, and paper clips to use this strategy.

Procedure

1. The students read their drafts aloud. Most students enjoy reading to a peer with whom they are comfortable.

2. The students then cut apart their drafts using scissors, so each sentence is on a separate small piece of paper.

3. Encourage them to rearrange their sentences by moving them into different positions. They can experiment with a variety of orders. Once they have made their adjustments, they use paper clips to secure the new arrangement of sentences to a blank page.

4. The students read their revised organization to their peer partner. They discuss whether the revision helps the organization and clarifies their ideas for their audience.

5. On a clean sheet of paper, students copy new drafts from their sentences secured with paper clips. They can also add more ideas and transitions at this time.

6. The students share their revised draft with a peer, their teacher, or their parents.

Teaching Tip

Many teachers demonstrate the *Snip 'n' Clip* strategy using a document camera and projecting the process on a screen. Students see how sentences can be reorganized and how the rearrangement clarifies ideas and strengthens the draft.

Computer savvy writers naturally do *Snip 'n' Clip* when they are drafting a document using a word processor. They use the cut and paste functions to move their sentences around, add more information, or delete what is not needed. My former junior high school reluctant writers often felt that it was easier to draft and rewrite on a computer.

An Example of Student Revision

Carlos's original draft

My favorite holiday is x-mas because I like the snow and the presents. I spend time with my family in x-mas in my house and in the park playing with the snow. We like to have fun every day on x-mas.

When my dad said that he is going to talk to Santa is so funny because we stay in the car and he go inside of Walmart and he think that I don't know Santa don't exist but I already told him that I know he is not real but he still can buy me things and I love x-mas.

My x-mas tree looks cool because it have a lot of colorful lights and pictures. We eat lobster it taste good with rice and green beans and I like x-mas because we have fun and we eat things we like.

Carlos's teacher read his three paragraphs and asked him to "snip" apart the three paragraphs. She asked him to think about reorganizing them. Carlos decided that paragraph 1 and paragraph 3 should be together, because they both described Christmas, whereas paragraph 2 was a specific Santa story.

Carlos's revised draft

My favorite holiday is Christmas because I like the snow and the presents. I spend time with my family on Christmas in my house and in the park playing with my friends in the snow. We like to have fun every day of our Christmas vacation.

My Christmas tree looks cool because it has strings of colorful lights and ornaments. We eat lobster that tastes so good with rice and green beans. I like Christmas because we eat things we like and have fun.

Last Christmas my dad said that he was going to talk to Santa. Dad is so funny because we stay in the car and he went inside Walmart. He thinks that I don't know that Santa doesn't really exist, but I already told him that I know he is not real. Dad can still buy me things and I love Christmas.

16

Tally Up

Focus

Varying the length and style of sentences is a sophisticated skill for many students. Sentence Variety (one of the 6 Traits) is often difficult to teach, and for many writers, difficult to learn. In *Tally Up,* the goal is to reduce the number of same first words without changing the ideas or purpose of the writing. Students will need to know how to **combine sentences**, start a sentence with a **phrase or clause,** or **reposition a sentence.** Note that this strategy is least useful for poetry or song lyrics, where a repetitive sentence structure is often desirable and part of the crafting of the piece.

Procedure

1. Students circle the first word in every sentence on their drafts.

2. Along the margins of their drafts, students tally how many times each word was used as the first word of a sentence. (They draw hash marks to indicate how many times each first word was used.)

3. Students decide which first words to change based on the number of times the same first words were used.

4. Students revise their sentences, but not the focus of their writing, and keep in mind their purpose and audience.

5. Students reread for clarity and organization once they have revised all the marked words they chose. Once the sentence beginnings are revised, the order of the sentences may need to be altered.

An Example of Student Revision

Wendy's original draft

I have always felt at a loss when it comes to revision. I remember my sophomore composition class where the teacher brought me to tears each time I conferenced with her at her desk for a one-on-one conference. **My** papers were marked to shreds and she didn't ever say much. I would see comments in the margins like: How? What? Why? **But** I was not armed with a single strategy to answer these questions.

Wendy's revised draft

I remember my sophomore composition class where my teacher brought me to tears every time I met with her at her desk for one-on-one conference. **My** papers were marked to shreds but she rarely said a word. **Questions** like, How? What? and Why? jump out at me from the margins. **Terror** raged through my entire self. **Confusion**, frustration and anger built up inside me all because I had not been armed with a single strategy to attack these questions.

PART IV

Focus on Voice, Word Choice, and Sentence Fluency

Words on Writing From Pam Muñoz Ryan

During the earlier stages of a novel, I reread and rewrite the manuscript from the beginning of the first chapter every day. That approach feels organic to me—this recursive writing. Of course, once the story progresses to a longer length, I don't always continue to do that every time I sit down to work, but I do it often. I don't impose any word count or number-of-hours quota on myself, or have any rules, except one: persistence. Nothing glamorous. No dramatic epiphanies. Just revisiting and rewriting. For me, momentum is far more important than inspiration.

To revise for voice, word choice, and sentence fluency (sometimes collectively referred to as style) is not a simple process. The voice of a draft needs to reflect the purpose and audience of the writing, and writers need to make decisions based on their understanding of the writing prompt or assignment. Voice is not a simple task of writing the same way a person talks; it's an important indication of tone and mood. The revision strategy, *Create an Authentic Voice*, gives students guidance about how to write with their own individual voice, and helps show them the function of audience in determining the voice for a particular piece.

Word choice is a delicate balance that subtly reveals the writer's bias, opinions, likes, and dislikes. In the revision strategy *Verbs! Get Some*, the writer chooses verbs that best create a picture with words. In the revision strategy *Using Wordle*, which involves an Internet tool as a "wordsmith," overused words are highlighted. Students recognize the overused words and are encouraged to replace them to enhance their drafts. Revising for word choice is about selecting the best word for the situation and meaning of their drafts.

In both the *Write Less, Write More* and *Sentence Fluency* revision strategies, students are urged to write compound, complex, or compound–complex sentences and to vary the length of their sentences in order to create fluency in their drafts. Students should read their drafts aloud to listen for fluency and to determine which sentences should be revised for length or complexity.

The Revision Strategies in Part IV Correlated to the 6 Traits of Effective Writing

Strategy/6 Traits	Ideas	Organization	Voice	Word Choice	Sentence Fluency
Create Authentic Voice			•	•	•
Write Less, Write More	•			•	•
Wordle	•			•	•
Sentence Fluency					•
Verbs! Get Some			•	•	

Note: Since the revision strategies do not address Conventions, this trait is not represented in this chart.

17

Create Authentic Voice

Focus

Students analyze and revise their own drafts to determine if they have been able to establish an authentic voice. Additional ideas, organization, and word choice all have an impact on voice.

Procedure

1. Read aloud a selection of published or student writing as a clear example of authentic voice and discuss the factors that make the writer's style distinctive. Explain that voice is the writer's unique way of expressing ideas and emotions and that effective use of voice gives writing personality. The selection below from the novel *Speak* provides an example of a unique voice.

Welcome to Merry Weather High

It is my first morning of high school. I have seven new notebooks, a skirt I hate and a stomachache.

    The school bus wheezes to my corner. The door opens and I step up. I am the first pickup of the day. The driver pulls away from the curb while I stand in the aisle. Where to sit? I've never been a backseat wastecase. If I sit in the middle, a stranger could sit next to me. If I sit in the front it will make me look like a little kid but I figure it's the best chance I have to make eye contact with one of my friends, if any of them have decided to talk to me yet.

Source: Anderson, 1999, p. 3.

2. Have students read their drafts aloud, to a partner or to themselves. As they do so, they should be considering the following:

   - Can I hear my voice?
   - Is there personality in the draft?

3. Next, ask students to consider the intended reader of the piece. Explain that knowing the audience for the piece will determine what voice to use. For example, a writer can use familiar language when writing to a peer or certain family members but may need to be more formal when writing a school paper or to an older, more reserved family member.

   - Who is the audience?
   - What form of voice should be used? Familiar? Formal?
   - Is there any unacceptable language in the draft? Vulgarity is rarely acceptable in writing; know your audience well before using any vulgarity.
   - What is the overall feeling conveyed in the draft? Share the draft with a peer or peer group to learn their interpretations and feelings when they read the draft.

4. Students can read their drafts aloud multiple times, as they consider any or all of the following aspects of voice:

   - Is the opening as strong and full of interest as the closing?
   - Do all the sentences and paragraphs have the same voice?
   - Is the language natural and sincere? Avoid trite expressions, as they weaken the draft; use more natural and sincere language to strengthen the draft.
   - Are the word choices clear? Avoid clichés (overused comparisons no longer used), as they give the reader little to think about and may be confusing; use clearer word choices to convey the ideas in the draft.
   - Are there different levels of interest in the draft? Does the draft have real authority when making a point? Does the draft show interest or passion when expressing an opinion? Avoid a voice that is predictable, showing the same level of enthusiasm no matter what the content.
   - Does the draft hold the reader's attention? Is there a level of commitment? Is it honest and interesting?

18

Write More, Write Less

Focus

Many students begin their writing with a telegraphic style, jumping from idea to idea without connecting the dots. Others include an excessive level of detail or description and lose the thread of meaning that renders the details relevant and clear. In this strategy, students first revise their drafts by expanding an original sentence. Then they revise by shortening their original sentences. This strategy helps students think about how to expand ideas and how to tighten their writing. The teacher's guidance helps students identify where one or the other technique is needed: when to write more and when to write less.

Procedure

Write More

1. Have students read through their drafts to find brief, short sentences, and then choose one to expand. For example, "The dog was making noises over there."

2. Ask students to revise the sentence by adding as many words as possible without significantly changing the meaning. Examples of rewritten sentences include the following:

   - A black and tan beagle was barking behind the garage.
   - The brown and black German shepherd was howling in the driveway.
   - Gertie, a tan and white colored collie, was barking and snapping at a cat that had run up a tree in the back yard.

> **Teaching Tip**
>
> Sometimes the revised sentences can become *too* full of words and details, but for this part of the strategy that is fine—students are experimenting and brainstorming with expanding sentences and ideas.

Write Less

1. Have students read through their drafts to find a long sentence. This could possibly be the longest sentence in the draft.

2. Guide the students as they revise by eliminating all possible words to take the sentence down to a much shorter sentence without changing its meaning. For example, the long sentence:

   - The class of twenty-six students was having an afternoon picnic at the abandoned park on the top of the mountain; they were interrupted when the dark clouds gathered and rain came slashing down on their food and fun.

   could be revised as follows:

   - A mountaintop thunderstorm ruined the class picnic.

Variations

1. Change sentence length by removing or adding details.

   - Direct students to read through their drafts and choose a long sentence.
   - Have students rewrite that sentence, without significantly changing the meaning, to a much shorter sentence.
   - Once this sentence is written, they lengthen the sentence again, this time using different details.

2. Expand a brief sentence by combining it with another sentence.

   - Have students read through their drafts and choose a brief sentence.
   - Have students attach that sentence to another sentence in the draft—most likely the sentence immediately before or after it.
   - Once the sentences are attached or combined, have students rewrite the new, longer sentence so it is smoother.

3. Collaborate with a partner to change the length of a sentence. This variation allows students to work together with an audience and gain ideas about ways to revise and improve the initial sentences.

   - Have students read through their drafts and choose a long (or a brief) sentence to share with a partner.
   - The partners then revise each other's sentences, shortening long sentences or lengthening brief ones.

Teaching Tip

For this strategy, it's best to first model the procedure with the whole class. Here is a possible format to follow:

1. Display a short sentence for the whole class to see on a whiteboard, blackboard, overhead projector, or computer screen. Example: *The dog was making noises over there.*

2. Have students rewrite the sentence, without changing the meaning, by expanding and adding details.

3. Read some of the new sentences to the class so that they hear different versions of the sentence and many possibilities for changing it.

4. Display a long sentence for the whole class to see. Example: *The thirteen students were eating at a table in the corner of the dark, noisy cafeteria when the announcement was made for students to return to their classrooms to begin the next period of the day; the students gathered their books and returned to their classrooms.*

5. Have students rewrite the sentence to make it as short as possible without changing the basic meaning. Example: *The students left the cafeteria and returned to their classrooms upon hearing the announcement.*

6. Read several student examples to show the class many possibilities.

Examples of Students' Revisions

Garrett's original short sentence

Wear safety goggles, gloves, and make sure you use an outdoor location.

Garrett's revised sentence (write more)

Wear safety goggles, gloves, and make sure you use an outdoor location; for example, your driveway would work perfectly.

Garrett's original long sentence

When we opened the doors connecting to the park, the heat flooded out and washed over us—the park was not only indoors, but it was also heated to 83 degrees; that day and the next we had the time of our lives.

Garrett's revised sentence (write less)

After we arrived at the indoor park, we discovered it was heated to 83 degrees!

19

Wordle

Focus

Wordle is an online tool that creates *word clouds* from the drafts students have written. The clouds produced give prominence to words in the drafts based on how often the students have used them. Students revise by entering their drafts into the Wordle website (on the Internet). They examine the visual results that focus on word choice.

Procedure

1. Students access the website www.wordle.net.

2. Click on the Create tab, and a box opens, in which the students enter all or parts of their drafts.

3. Students may type their entire drafts into the box, depending on the length.

4. If a multipage draft becomes cumbersome, encourage students to experiment by typing in just one or several paragraphs.

5. When the text is in the box, students click GO, just below the lower left corner of the box.

6. The result is a *word cloud*, which is a random configuration of the words typed.

7. The more a word has been used, the larger it appears in the cloud. Students immediately discover whether they have overused certain words.

8. Students can also use the Edit, Language, Font, Layout, and Color tabs to create an infinite number of versions of their word clouds.

9. Once students finish generating their word clouds, they can print them.

10. Students revise their drafts by changing words, deleting words, or adding more ideas based on what they have learned from the word clouds.

An Example of Student Use of Wordle

Brian's original draft

The rush you feel as your throwing someone through the air. The pain you feel as you're getting choked. The success you feel as your getting a new bolt. The pure joy you feel as your standing on the podium and receiving a medal. The name of this emotional rollercoaster is Judo.

Judo is a full contact sport that was created in Japan by Dr. Jigro Kano. It's a sport that is very physical but also very technical. It is a physical sport because you have to be able to be thrown and still get up. Judo is a technical sport because if you use the right technique no matter how large your opponent is you can throw him onto the ground. That is why Judo is a very technical and physical sport.

Now that you know about Judo, I think you should sign up for it. It is rather easy to sign up for Judo; All you have to do is go to a dojo (a place where judo is taught). You can come to sign up anytime of the year. The only issue is that it might be only be open everyday of the week.

Judo would also be a good thing to sign up for because of the fact that it teaches you self-defense. Judo is also gets you in great shape because you do a lot of sparring (fighting) involved witch is a great way to work out and have fun. Those are the physical aspects of Judo.

Judo is a very easy sport to sign up for. It's also a great way to learn self defense and workout. You will also have a lot of fun doing it. That is why I think you should join Judo.

Brian's *word cloud* from his original draft.

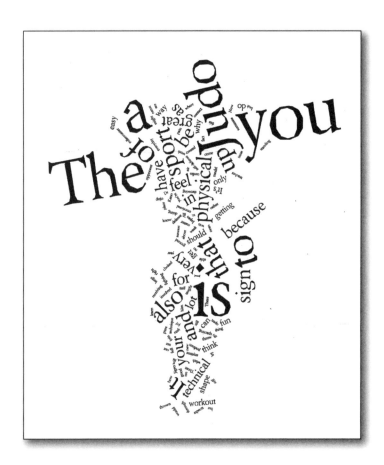

20

Sentence Fluency

Focus

Sentence fluency is like a string of pearls—all the pearls need to be connected seamlessly and be in harmony with each other. For students to write with sentence fluency, they need to be taught to internalize grammar concepts.

Definitions

Compound Sentence: A compound sentence is two simple sentences joined by a comma and a conjunction such as *and, but, or, so, for,* or *yet.*

- Student example: Geoff, Gordon, and Traci wrote, "The wolverines were hungry, and my face looked particularly appetizing."

Complex Sentence: A complex sentence includes one independent clause and one or more dependent clauses beginning with such words as *because, when,* or *who.*

- Student example: Geoff, Gordon, and Traci wrote, "Dodging wolverines proved difficult when wearing snowshoes in 15 inches of powder."

Compound–Complex Sentence: A compound–complex sentence contains two or more independent clauses and *one* or more dependent clauses.

- Student example: Geoff, Gordon, and Traci wrote, "The wolverines, despite their heavy paws, were surprisingly swift, and as I fell they captured me, the only woman in the group."

Source: Sebranek, Kemper, & Meyer, 2010, p. 83.

Procedure

1. Teachers model the three following approaches to combining sentences, and remind their students that when they combine sentences, the original meaning, purpose, and voice of the writing should be retained:

   - Combining sentences to create a compound sentence.
   - Combining sentences to create a complex sentence.
   - Combining sentences to create a compound–complex sentence.

2. Students identify their simple sentences (independent clauses) by underlining them in their drafts.

3. Students combine two simple sentences to create a compound sentence.

4. Students combine a simple sentence with a dependent clause (sentence fragment) to create a complex sentence.

5. Students combine two or more independent clauses (simple sentences) with a dependent clause (sentence fragment) to create a compound–complex sentence.

6. Students read their drafts aloud and mark, with two slashes at the end of the sentence, each time they stumble or need to reread. These stumblings indicate a lack of sentence fluency.

21

Verbs! Get Some

Focus

Active verbs are among the powerful tools that enable writers to create pictures with words and allow readers to visualize what they are reading. "The more specific the verb, the more energy and specificity the sentence will have" (Heard, 2002, p. 86). Though this strategy requires writers to use more specific nouns and more precise verbs, it is not intimidating, because the new word choices can be selected at the student's own level of vocabulary and understanding. For example, a phrase with specific verbs might read as follows: *Jada rebounded, dribbled, and shot and scored,* as opposed to *she ran down the basketball court.* It's all in the verb choice.

Procedure

1. Students circle all the verbs in their drafts with colored ink or pencil. They may work with a partner to locate all their verbs, depending on their age and ability level.

2. Students identify "to be" verbs (am, is, are, was, were, be, being, been) with another color. (Student writers have a tendency to overuse "to be" verbs, which makes their sentences more static and less descriptive.)

3. Create a word wall to provide the students with examples of strong verbs, such as verbs that can stand alone without the help of an adverb and verbs that show rather than tell. To best support students, try creating multiple verb word walls, so there is a different word wall for each specific writing assignment or genre. (Typically, teachers create walls of words that are overused or words to be avoided, but this doesn't help students who are in need of better verb choices.)

4. Together, students brainstorm vivid verbs to replace the weaker verbs. They work with partners or in small groups to share their new verb choices and decide whether the new verb creates the scene or image they want to convey.

Teaching Tip

Teachers should review verbs with their students and model, using a student's paper, how to identify the verbs. Since many students have difficulty identifying verbs, this strategy is more effective when used in pairs.

PART V

Two Heads Are Better Than One:
Peer Conference

Words on Writing From Michael Salinger

Reading a piece out loud is a very important part of my revision process. Rolling the words around, taking them for a test spin is the quickest and easiest way for me to assess the flow and rhythm of whatever I am working on. Saying the words out loud, whether to another person or simply into the air of my office, catches those mistakes made during the rush of a first draft. Reading out loud also helps with the creation of text, I will speak what I have already produced in order to "find out what comes next"—often times the next line just appears because I have taken the time to stop and read what I have already committed to page. So, it seems, revision needn't wait until the end of the writing process and speaking the lines out loud is a technique that will work at any point of composition.

E ven though writing is a solitary act, all writers benefit from working with a partner or small group of readers who respond to their drafts and give them significant feedback. Peer response is not an editing but a revision process, in which peers respond to the writer's draft while thinking about these types of questions: What did I like about the draft? What don't I understand about the draft? What additional information is needed?

The four revision strategies in this section—*SMART, Draw as a Way to Rethink, Pointing,* and *Marathon*—all call for peers to listen to a writer's draft in a nonjudgmental frame of mind and respond to it in a thoughtful, meaningful way. Concrete, substantial responses provide the writers not only with additional details but also revision suggestions that could improve their drafts. All revision strategies benefit from peer response, but we've chosen these particular strategies for this section because they illustrate well the advantage that can be gained by working with a partner or small group.

The Revision Strategies in Part V Correlated to the 6 Traits of Effective Writing

Strategy/6 Traits	Ideas	Organization	Voice	Word Choice	Sentence Fluency
SMART	•	•	•	•	•
Draw as a Way to Rethink	•	•			
Marathon Writing	•				
Pointing	•		•	•	

Note: Since the revision strategies do not address Conventions, this trait is not represented in this chart.

22

SMART

Focus

Many middle school and high school students can multitask as they revise their drafts; they look at their word choices and decide if better words could be substituted, if ideas should be moved to aid organization, if more information needs to be added to clarify or support their topics, and if any parts should be removed because they present extraneous information not needed in the draft. In order to help college students revise and think about these tasks, Faigley and Witte (1981) coined the acronym ARMS (Add, Remove, Move, Substitute). Kelly Gallagher, a high school literacy teacher in California, coined his own acronym, STAR (Substitute, Take things out, Add, Rearrange) to help his students revise (Gallagher, 2006).

These are both fine acronyms for a revision process that results in revised and greatly improved compositions. We decided, however, to add one more important step to these tasks; that is, *thinking* about each decision made with audience and purpose in mind. Hence, the SMART acronym. Today, through instruction, direction, and conferencing with teachers and peers, many middle and high school students revise their drafts implementing all or some combination of the strategies represented by the SMART acronym.

S – Substitute better words for those in the draft.

M – Move ideas, sentences, and/or paragraphs to help organize the draft.

A – Add more details to clarify the draft; add dialogue to strengthen the voice of the draft; add more information to the draft; add figurative language to make the writing more visual.

R – Remove any ideas that detract from the meaning of the draft.

T – Think about each of these revision decisions with purpose and audience in mind.

Procedure

1. Students revise their drafts, thinking specifically about substituting words, moving ideas, adding new details, and removing unnecessary information.

2. Students first work on this procedure independently and then share in pairs. They may also request their teacher's input. Once the students have completed their revisions based on the SMART set of questions, they share their revised essay with a fellow student before turning it in.

An Example of Student Revision

The student example below is taken from Mrs. Batt's twelfth-grade English composition class. After students complete their first drafts, each student completes a self-critique sheet, a peer conference, and a teacher conference. The self-critique activity sheet has guiding questions related to "show, don't tell," figurative language, anecdotes, dialogue, and audience/purpose. (Examples of both the self-critique sheet and the peer conferencing revision sheet are at the end of this strategy.) Following the self-critique and student collaboration, the students revise their essays with SMART.

Lacey's original third paragraph

When my father died a few months later, the bear became a way to keep him with me even though he was gone. I would talk to it, as if it were him, telling it about my days, school, and life. **Years later when I talked about it with my mom, she made me cry again because she said it was the hardest thing she ever had to watch** (Removed from revised essay).

Lacey's original final paragraph

Weeks later when we were finally allowed back inside to salvage lost items, my bear was found dirty and damp but intact. After the fire, I never talked to my bear again. **After losing my father for the second time, I knew he was never coming back** (Moved to a new paragraph). **But I know now that the memories of him are the thread that's keeping the bear together** (Substituted different words in the revised essay).

Lacey's revised third paragraph

When my father died **in a car crash** (Added a new detail) a few months later, the bear became a way to keep him with me even though he was gone. I would talk to it, as if it were him, telling it about my days, school, and life. **Every night before I went to bed, I'd sit at the bottom bunk and hold the bear. Stroking the white fur I'd recall the most important moments of my day, "Today I got to go to Cousin Kara's house, and I got to see her get off her school bus, and Aunt Nancy took us to this playground that looked like a castle! It was so big; and we played for a really long time." Then I would tuck it into the covers next to me, kiss it good night, and say, "I love you, daddy"** (Added new details—figurative language and dialogue).

Lacey's revised final two paragraphs

Weeks later we were finally allowed back inside to salvage lost items **from the burnt and boarded up home**. (Added new details). My bear was found **on the floor of our bedroom** (Added new details), it was dirty and damp but intact. **They cleaned the bear, but they couldn't get rid of the smell of burning paper from its body. The fur is no longer soft either, it felt course and unwelcoming. When they gave me back the bear, I felt nothing. I was empty, just like the bear; there was no part of my father left inside of me either** (Added new details—figurative language).

I never talked to my bear again after the fire; **I don't even keep it in my room** (Added a new detail). After losing my father for the second time, I knew he was never coming back. **It became harder to face, and I didn't need the bear as a reminder of that. But every now and then when I see the bear in our pink basement I'll pick it up, just to think of him, and just sit and stroke the damaged fur** (Added new details). It's only now that I **realized** (Substituted for know) that it's the memories of him that are the thread that's keeping **me** (Added detail to clarify), and the bear, together.

Descriptive Essay Self-Critique

Name _____

1. Write down your most effective example of SDT (show, don't tell).

2. Write down your favorite example of a simile or metaphor in your essay.

3. Do you use an anecdote (a short, meaningful story) in your essay?
   Discuss the insight/understanding your audience will gain from your anecdote. If you don't have one, think of one, and add it to this sheet right now; then consider adding it to your descriptive essay.

4. Where is dialogue used most effectively? What does it reveal about the character and situation? Again, if no dialogue is present, create it below, and show where you plan to incorporate it in your descriptive essay.

5. What is the overall purpose of your essay? What should your reader take from this descriptive essay?

Source: Mrs. Jennifer Batt, high school English teacher and head of the English department, Stroudsburg Area School District, Stroudsburg, Pennsylvania.

Descriptive Essay Peer Response

Name of Reviewer _____

Author of Descriptive Essay _____

1. Is the title creative and subjective? Why or why not?

2. Suggest an alternate title after reading the entire piece.

3. Does the author get your attention in the introduction? How? What can be done to improve the introduction?

4. Does this essay contain interesting sensory description? Write down an example of the essay's most effect SDT (show, don't tell) moment.

5. Does this essay contain any similes and metaphors? Write an example of one. Is it a cliché?

6. Does the writer's voice or personality come through? What do we learn about the writer?

7. Does this essay strike an emotional chord in the reader? What emotion?

8. Make a few grammatical, spelling, word choice, punctuation, or tense corrections on the draft itself. If there are no corrections needed, please note this below.

9. What grade do you think this essay has earned?

_____

Source: Mrs. Jennifer Batt, high school English teacher and head of the English department, Stroudsburg Area School District, Stroudsburg, Pennsylvania.

23

Draw as a Way to Rethink

Focus

Students draw, independently or with a peer, as a way to rethink their drafts. A lack of organization or scant use of details in the draft results in a sparse drawing. Drawing is a good way to make the shape of a piece visual, and it allows students to spot problems—literally, to see them—when a rereading of the written words might not provide the same insights. Students have used this method on state assessments when they are not allowed to collaborate on their writing.

Procedure

Independent Method

1. Have students reread their drafts with blank paper in front of them.

2. Tell students they will now be visualizing either the whole draft or a part of it. (Some teachers will find it important to give time limits, so students don't spend an overwhelming amount of time on this step, visualizing, or on the next step, drawing.)

3. Students draw on the blank paper what they see in their drafts. Their drawings can take one of three forms:

   • *One large image (a mural with details):* Using this method, students can label parts of the mural, extend their thinking about one part of the draft, see where parts are lacking, and compare the drawing with the draft to see if the draft is lacking or if it is successful.

- *A paper filled with a random assortment of images (many details from the draft):* This method is successful for students who go through the draft and find concrete details. It is also a way for students to visually brainstorm more details to be added to the draft.
- *A story board or a story line:* This method can be used for narrative, persuasive, or informative writing, as the order of the draft can fit nicely into the story board, or it can show the student how the order does not flow. By using a story board to draw the order and details of the draft, students can see where new information is needed and can identify holes in their thinking and their writing.

4. Students add details to their drawings. The quality of the drawing is not the issue; the quality of the visual details and thoughts is important. If a drawing has only a few details, students rethink and add more details to the drawing.

5. The new details do not always have to be drawings. Students can add words and phrases and sentences to their drawings to further explain and identify their ideas. These words, phrases, and sentences can come from the draft, or they can be new. The purpose is to add to the thinking and the draft.

6. Students then incorporate these visual details from their drawings into their drafts.

Peer Method

1. Students read their drafts to peers.

2. Peers draw what they visualize while listening to the draft.

3. Peers draw using one of the following forms:
   - one large image
   - several images randomly
   - a grid as a story line

4. Peers' drawings must visually represent the written ideas.

5. Peers' drawings can be labeled with words, phrases, and sentences.

6. Student and peers discuss the drawings and the draft. This strategy works well for visual learners to rethink and revise their drafts.

Variation

In any of the drawings (one large image, many small details, or a grid), adding dialogue is a way to enhance the revised draft. It's particularly easy to add dialogue balloons to story lines. For the visual learner, this is a means to "see" the draft and add the spoken word.

Teaching Tip

This is a very creative way to have students rethink their drafts. The drawings can be posted around the room, with or without the final drafts. Students enjoy looking at other students' visuals for creative ideas, and they find it interesting to see how peers visualize their own writing. On a logistical note, some students can become so involved in their drawings that they lose track of time and don't return to their drafts. If teachers encourage drawing as a way to revise, they need to guide students and keep them aware of time constraints.

Examples of Student Drawings From a Draft

Mara's original draft

Teachers have classroom rules for many reasons. One reason is to help you and your fellow classmates have a good learning environment. Another reason is to help you learn the most. Lastly, it is to help keep you safe. For these three reasons this is why teachers have rules.

Rules in the classroom help not only you but your fellow students to learn. One of a teacher's biggest rules is being quiet. By being quiet it helps the teacher teach the most they can in their class. Also this helps students concentrate on their work. Raising your hand when you have a question is another big rule that teachers have. This helps teachers know what you aren't understanding. Also other students might have the same question and by having a quiet class teachers don't have to repeat themselves much.

Teachers have rules to help you. One example of this is no cheating. Cheating is not good. You don't learn anything from it. So in the long run cheating is just hurting yourself. Also respecting one another is a big rule. Learning how to respect others at an early age will help you for many years. It helps to make a good learning and, in the future, a good working environment.

Lastly, rules are to keep you safe. Such as not running down the halls. If you run down a hall you could injure yourself and perhaps others. Also being quiet during emergencies. You need to hear directions so you know what to do. These are just a few of the many rules there are to keep you safe.

Rules can be a pain, but they are for your interest. They help you and fellow students have a good learning environment. Also they help you specifically learn the most you can. Lastly, they help keep you and your peers safe.

Drawings by Mara, Kiki, and Maggie, as they visualize Mara's draft

Drawing by Mara, the student author.

Drawing by Maggie, a peer responder.

Drawing by Kiki, a peer responder.

24

Marathon Writing

Focus

Many students write drafts and recognize the need for revision but find it difficult to ask for ideas. They need an audience, but they are not ready for feedback. This may sound strange, but having an audience that listens intently can be a strong revision strategy in and of itself. A nonthreatening audience for an oral reading can give students a vehicle to determine the areas that need revision. This strategy, which is drawn from the National Writing Project model of a writing marathon (Louth, 2010), has been shown to be a successful way to give students this opportunity.

Procedure

1. Students write their drafts on topics of their choice if possible; otherwise, the draft may be a class assignment.

2. Students form groups of at least four or five.

3. Once the groups are formed, one writer reads his draft to the group without apology or qualification.

   - The draft may be read one or more times.
   - It is important that the writer not interject commentary into the reading, reading only what is on the paper.

4. The listeners may request the text be read a second time.

5. When the writer is finished reading, a simple "thank you" is enough to signal the end of the reading.

6. The audience has a responsibility during the reading to listen fully and attentively, without taking notes or writing, as their fellow student is reading.

7. At the end of the reading, the audience makes no comments.

8. When the first writer has finished reading, the next writer reads and the process repeats itself: oral reading, listening, and silence at the end.

9. This reading marathon allows writers to read their drafts to an audience and to consider their own words in the attentive silence of their "readers." The audience listens, and the writer, listening with them, thinks about areas needed for change.

Teaching Tip

Sometimes the drafts can be so long that it might be difficult for all the students in the group to finish in one class period. If this happens, the teacher might want to announce a maximum length of time for each reader. Each writer in the group should be able to finish an oral reading of a draft in the given time period.

If time permits, have students come to the group prepared to write. The group, with proper supervision, can travel to a different place in the school or on the school grounds, and once situated, can collaboratively create a draft. With a proper amount of time, the resulting draft, whether narrative or explanatory/ informational, can be written and read, and the whole group can experience writing and reading to an audience.

25

Pointing

Focus

Many times students struggle with the content of their piece. They finish the draft and think the piece might be finished. They feel that the content is okay, or it might be a bit deficient, but they are not sure how to enhance it. When students are confronted with the need for more content, and they use peer conferencing as a means to expand their drafts, it is sometimes the ideas of their peers, rather than an expansion of their original thinking, that become incorporated into the writing. *Pointing* (Elbow & Belanoff, 1999) avoids that pitfall by having the writers' peers create a "pointing" list of the writer's own words and phrases in the draft that capture their attention and interest.

The advantage of this strategy is that the writer ends up with a list that serves as a direction; the writer also has a chance to slowly read the draft aloud and **listen** to the words. In addition, the writer receives immediate feedback. Finally, the reading and the feedback are nonjudgmental, which, for the high school writer, can be the difference between wanting to write more and revise, and wanting to give up.

Procedure

1. Guide the student into a peer conferencing situation. One or two peers work best for this strategy.

2. Have students decide if the whole or a portion of the draft needs examination for content.

3. The students who are the audience (the listeners) need papers and pencils to respond.

4. The student who has written the draft reads it to the audience, making no side comments; that is, the writer doesn't say things like, "I know this part is weak," or "This part is bad."

5. During the reading, the peers who are listening are jotting down words, phrases, and pieces of the draft that jump out at them. The success of this strategy relies on listeners recording words they find interesting. Emphasize that the students should not write phrases they "like" or "dislike" but instead should record words they find interesting or striking. The audience should make no comments, such as, "I really liked this part" or "You need more details in this part." At the end of the reading, the listeners continue jotting words and phrases that stuck in their memories.

6. When they have finished writing, the listeners hand their lists of words and phrases to the writer. These are the *pointing* words. A short list shows the writer that more development and content should be added. A long list shows the writer that the content and the details are sound, and it is now up to the writer to add more or leave it alone.

7. The writer can read over the list and decide if more details are needed.

Teaching Tip

This strategy is a good tool for parents who want to help. The student can take a draft home and ask any parent or guardian to be an audience and write words and phrases on a paper and hand it over. Some parents are daunted by high school writing, but any parent can help using this strategy.

Examples of Students' Pointing

Kiki's first draft

She left home in the morning. She walked on the road. With her was a pet. The weather was not so good. She missed the vehicle for school. While walking further she and the pet got lost. They got lost in the woods. The woods were scary. She saw a house. The house looked scary. She heard some sounds. She went inside the house. There she and the pet saw some scary things. Some scary things happened. They left the house. Scary things followed them. They went through the forest. They finally got home. Then they were safe. Or were they?

Pointing for the first draft

Responses from student #1:

With him was a pet

The woods were scary

On the road

Responses from student #2:

Road

Woods

Scary things

House

Kiki's revised draft

Mara was finally ready to leave for school. She put her boots on and carefully shut the front door behind her. Today was "bring your pet to school day," so Mara brought her hamster Tigger in his small, plastic cage. While she was walking down the sidewalk it began to rain. Within minutes it was thundering and lightening. She was almost to the corner when she saw her bus speed away. She began waving her arms around "WAIT! WAIT! Come back!" she yelled. She dropped her arms in defeat. She didn't have her cell phone, and her parents had already left for work. Her only choice was to walk to school.

Walking to school was one thing, but in a big storm! She decided to go through the woods to get out of the rain. With her backpack in one arm and Tigger's cage in the other, she trudged through the woods picking leaves and twigs off of her clothes. It didn't take long for her to get lost. All of the sudden she saw a dark figure pass her. Mara was getting very paranoid. Wanting to get as far away as possible, she broke into a sprint. While running, she tripped over a log. Tigger's cage fell to the ground and opened. Tigger ran out deeper into the woods.

Pointing for Kiki's revised draft

Responses from two students

Hamster Tigger in his small, plastic cage

Waving her arms to the bus

Trudged through the woods—got lost

Dark figure

Withering wood

Cold hand

Crack of thunder

A man weaving in between trees—same as before

Tripped over a log

PART VI

The Reading–Writing Connection:
Consult Quality Literature

Words on Writing From Jerry Spinelli

I write in the morning. The first thing I do each day is read aloud to myself what I wrote the previous day. Long before papyrus, language was invented for the ear. Imperfections unnoticed on the page can come to light when heard, like dust in a sunbeam. Also, hearing your words helps mimic the objectifying distance provided by putting your manuscript in a drawer for a month. Then, when the book is finished, I read the whole thing aloud.

W hen student writers competently use literary devices such as metaphors, similes, alliteration, and personification, they strengthen their drafts by clarifying their meaning for readers. The revision strategies *Paint a Picture With Words* and *Personification in Poetry* encourage students to use literary devices to enhance their drafts as part of their revision process.

Write From Another Point of View is a sophisticated strategy, since it requires thorough understanding of a different perspective. In this revision strategy, students are shown two pieces of literature, expressing two different points of view, from the same historical event. In order to write from another perspective, students may need to research and read more about a point of view that is not their own.

In the revision strategy *What Did You Say?* students are encouraged to add specific dialogue to the draft as well as content. Written effectively, dialogue can bring a character to life and move the narrative forward. The beginning of any draft is the hook, the motivation for the reader to read the draft; the ending, on the other hand, is crucial to how the reader interprets the draft. *Once Upon a Time* and *And They All Lived Happily Ever After* are revision strategies that give students a range of different types of beginnings and endings to consider, in order to help them construct their own.

All the strategies in this section involve elements of good writing that readers of quality literature will recognize. It is not a coincidence that professional writers are usually inveterate readers, since we all learn from our reading how ideas can be expressed effectively. It is very helpful for students to see the connections between reading and writing. You can help them make these connections by providing them with examples from different texts of the way other writers have crafted beginnings and endings, incorporated metaphors or dialogue, or represented an alternative perspective in their work.

The Revision Strategies in Part VI Correlated to the 6 Traits of Effective Writing

Strategy/6 Traits	Ideas	Organization	Voice	Word Choice	Sentence Fluency
Once Upon a Time	•	•			
And They All Lived Happily Ever After	•	•			
What Did You Say?	•		•	•	
Painting a Picture With Words	•	•	•	•	•
Personification in Poetry	•		•	•	•

Note: Since the revision strategies do not address Conventions, this trait is not represented in this chart.

26

Once Upon a Time

Focus

Beginnings are crucial to any draft. Readers need only to read the first sentence to determine if they want to read on. An effective beginning can show the logic and creativity that underlies the foundation for the whole draft. The key to an effective beginning lies in the arrangement of the ideas that will be explored in the draft.

Procedure

1. Students read the first sentence of a dozen or so books, magazine and/or newspaper articles, and textbooks to observe how other writers start their works.

2. Students discuss the first sentences they have read. What are their characteristics? What do they have in common?

3. Students make a list of the kinds of beginnings they observed and the text for each. (Complete citations for these Young Adult books can be found in the reference section.)

   - A quote: *Esperanza Rising* by Pam Munoz Ryan, *Chains* by Laurie Halse Anderson
   - An anecdote: *Island of the Blue Dolphins* by Scott O'Dell
   - Dialogue: *Number the Stars* by Lois Lowry
   - Vivid description of a scene: *A Wrinkle in Time* by Madeline L'Engle
   - Name of character: *The Lion, the Witch, and the Wardrobe* by C. S. Lewis, *Hatchet* by Gary Paulsen
   - Setting: *Hugo Cabret* by Brian Selznick
   - Action: *Savvy* by Ingrid Law, *Milkweed* by Jerry Spinelli
   - Emotion: *Where the Red Fern Grows* by Wilson Rawls
   - Figurative language: *Bridge to Terabithia* by Katherine Patterson

4. Students read over their drafts and think about which kind of beginning fits their purpose and audience best.

5. Students write two or three different beginnings for their drafts. Students then ask two or three peers which one they like best and why. Sometimes, a good beginning is buried in the second or third sentence of the first paragraph and needs only to be brought forward.

Teaching Tip

Have students select other texts to read from and have them identify the types of beginnings in those—they may need to add to the types and titles listed above.

An Example of Student Revision

Leslie's original beginning

Focusing on students' weaknesses tends to decrease their motivation and drive to improve their writing.

Leslie's revised beginning

As Colin perused his essay with a multitude of red teacher's marks, his heart sank, feeling quite defeated.

27

And They All Lived Happily Ever After

Focus

The ending to any piece of writing must obviously support the organization of the piece but can also help the reader to better understand the writer's ideas. The conclusion can reinforce the writer's voice and point of view, and make clear hopes for a brighter future or disappointment with reality. The ending can even be the start of another piece of writing, as with a serial publication. Endings are crucial to a well-written draft.

Procedure

1. Students read the last sentence in a dozen or so books, magazine and/or newspaper articles, and textbooks to observe how other writers end their work.

2. As with the effective beginnings, students discuss the endings they read, covering the similarities and differences they found in the endings. What surprised them about some of the endings? Which endings were predictable? Should endings only reiterate already stated information, or can they introduce new information? How do endings change depending on the genre of the writing? How do endings affect an entire piece?

3. Students make a list of the kinds of endings they read and the text for each. (Complete citations for each of these Young Adult books can be found in the reference section.)

   - Metaphor: *The Secret Life of Bees* by Sue Monk Kidd
   - Conclusion: *The Reader* by Bernhard Schlink
   - Lesson learned: *A Lesson Before Dying* by Ernest J. Gaines
   - Acceptance: *To Kill a Mockingbird* by Harper Lee

- Inspirational: *The Watsons Go to Birmingham—1963* by Christopher Paul Curtis
- Tear jerker: *The Ties That Bind, Ties That Break* by Lensey Namioka
- Hint to the future—it is not over: *Push (Precious)* by Sapphire
- Repeats title to show full circle: *The Hour I First Believed* by Walter Lamb
- Shows hope: *Fallen Angels* by Walter Dean Myers
- Emotional: *House on Mango Street* by Sandra Cisneros
- Ironic closure: *Lovely Bones* by Alice Sebold
- Cathartic: *One True Thing* by Anna Quindlen
- Dream fulfilled: *A Raisin in the Sun* by Lorraine Hansberry

4. Students reread their drafts and think about which ending works best with their drafts.

5. Students write two or three different endings for their drafts and then ask two or three peers which one they like best and why. Sometimes a good ending is a line in the draft. Remind students to keep that in mind as they reread their drafts.

Teaching Tip

Have students select other texts to read and have them identify the types of endings in those—they may need to add to the types and titles listed above. Teachers often need to provide models of good endings and have students in class share endings from books they have read as well.

28

What Did You Say?

Focus

Sometimes, students' personal narratives tell a story without inviting us in. Their stories may be just a listing of events that lack dynamics, making them monotonous and boring to read. This strategy breathes life into such initial drafts. When dialogue is added, the stories come alive.

Procedure

1. Choose a favorite passage that has strong dialogue to read aloud to the class. One of my favorites is the opening lines of *Eggs* by Jerry Spinelli. I particularly like to share this model, because it has the dialogue interwoven with the text. For illustrative purposes, I project the page on a document camera.

"I don't even like eggs," David said.
   "It's not just eggs," said his grandmother.
   "So what is it?" He no longer bothered to trim the surliness from his voice when speaking to her. (Spinelli, 2007, p. 1)

2. While students reread their drafts, use these questions to suggest they try inserting dialogue:

   - What other information, either facts or details, can be added through dialogue?
   - Where does dialogue need to be placed to give a vivid picture of the scene?
   - Does the dialogue reflect the authentic voice of the characters?

3. Through collaboration and peer conferencing, students decide where to place dialogue to strengthen the draft.

Teaching Tip

Once the drafts are revised, have an editing conversation about the following conventions governing dialogue:

- Quotation marks indicate words that are spoken.
- The first letter of the spoken word is capitalized.
- Dialogue tags (e.g., "said his grandmother") explain who is speaking.
- Dialogue tags can be positioned before, during, or after the spoken words.
- A new paragraph indicates a new speaker.

Examples of Students' Revisions

Sarah's original beginning

When I first became an independent reader, I frequently checked out the same book: an abridged version of *The Wizard of Oz.* I particularly remember this event, because our librarian had to have it delivered from another elementary school in the district.

Sarah's revised beginning

"Sarah," Mrs. Elliot, our librarian, sighed, "we'll have to have it brought over from the Franklin Elementary . . . again. Isn't there anything else you want to check out?"

"Oh, right, well, um, I can wait, but I guess while I wait. . . ." I ran away for a minute into the book stacks. "Can I check out this one until my other book comes?"

Danica's fourth paragraph

A decent sized room makes the extended visit a bit more tolerable. The bed sits right smack in the middle of the room against the back wall. To its left, a couch attached to the floor which also works like a bed, lies against the window, the most interesting and potentially creative aspect of the room. Your window acts as your easel. With a smidgen of imagination and some window markers, whatever mood exists inside you on any particular day could be expressed with the stroke of your hand. Looking past the possibilities, other windows across the way that belong to other rooms already have their own personalities. Rainbows, people, hearts, doodles, names, handprints and everything in between make the only realms to the outside world nearly impossible to see through.

Danica's revised paragraph

A decent sized room makes an extended visit a bit more tolerable. The bed sits right smack in the middle of the room against the back wall. To the left, the most interesting and unique aspect of the room, the window. The window does not only serve as a window to the main lobby, but as a window that lets patients express themselves and show their creativity while they remain trapped in their hospital rooms.

Markers upon markers of all different colors were sitting beside the window thanks to my nurses and visitors. I have seen other rooms decorated with these, but never thought of doing it myself. I saw the markers and decided to draw. I used the couch to reach higher up, making sure I covered the whole thing.

"Wow! That looks amazing! You have the best window in this whole hospital." I would hear doctors and nurses tell me all the time. I felt awesome knowing my art left them feeling good too. I could draw if I felt happy, or if I felt like crying. Drawing on my giant easel kept me sane.

29

Paint a Picture With Words

Focus

Sometimes, students' beginning drafts are dry and bland, even though they have written down the content that was important to them. With guidance and collaboration during the revision process, they are able to add alliteration, similes, and metaphors to enliven their drafts. Giving students excellent models, instruction, and practice with "word painting" can help them transform their bland descriptions into colorful passages for their audience.

Definitions

Review the definitions of alliteration, similes and metaphors with students.

Alliteration: Repeating the first consonant sound in three or more words ("soggy sneakers splashed").

Simile: An explicit comparison of two unlike objects using *like* or *as*. ("She looked like the unopened bud of a tulip.")

Metaphor: An implicit comparison of two unlike objects, not using *like* or *as* but instead using a term or phrase for one item that is usually applied to something else. ("'Careful, Shrimp,' Darren brayed.")

Procedure

1. Read aloud a favorite passage that contains alliteration, similes, and metaphors. One illustrative passage that I have shared is the beginning of *Framed* by Gordon Korman. The opening lines could be projected on a document camera:

A clammy rain misted down on the six hundred and eighty students assembled in ranks on the muddy front lawn of Cedarville Middle School. **Soggy sneakers splashed** as the principal led his students through twenty jumping jacks, bellowing encouragement through a megaphone.

2. Following the modeling, the students thoughtfully reread each paragraph of their drafts, thinking about their word choice and descriptions of the content—considering, for example, the following:

  • Is there a way to use a metaphor or simile to create a picture of your character?
  • Could alliteration or simile be used to make the setting more vivid?

3. Working independently or in collaboration with a peer, students revise their drafts by inserting alliteration, similes, and metaphors where appropriate.

4. The students share their revisions with a peer, teacher, or parent before the descriptive narrative is turned in.

Examples of Students' Revisions

Jason's original introduction

The development of my literacy history is a rocky, but yet a genuine description of the boy who barely read throughout the upper elementary and most of my high school years.

Jason's revised introduction

Rocky, Rough, Rambunctious. How does one describe his literacy history? My life of reading has been **like traversing across the Rockies.** If you dare, enter into the mind of this non-reader and watch how he has transformed into a reading maniac.

Max's original draft

Some people fall to the ground, because of the slippery ice. Outside you can see a group of teenagers standing there, grabbing in a bag and lighting fireworks. One of the teenagers is me. The adults also started to use fireworks and New Year's Eve rockets. The sky gets bright. Beautiful colors fill the sky, red, blue, green, almost every color and shape made the night feel like the day. Perfectly clean looking snow surrounded the street in this little village. It looked like nobody would even dare to touch it. It doesn't feel really cold outside anymore. Fireworks and alcohol made everybody warm. The air filled with the smell of cigarettes and fireworks compared to a typically New Year's Eve smell. But then a little mistake. I hear and smell a fireworks flying in our group, hits the head of a friend of mine. The fireworks fall on the ground.

Max's revised draft

Some people fall to the ground, because of the slippery ice. Outside you can see a group of teenagers standing there, taking fireworks out of a bag and lighting them. One of the teenagers is me. The adults also start to use fireworks and New Year's Eve rockets. The sky gets bright. Beautiful colors fill the sky, red, blue, green, almost every color and shape made the night feel like the day. Perfectly clean looking snow surrounded the street in this little village. It looked like nobody would even dare to touch it. It doesn't feel cold outside anymore. Fireworks and alcohol made everybody warm. The air filled with the smell of fireworks, typically for a New Year's Eve smell. But then a little mistake. I hear and smell a firework flying into our group, which hits the head of a friend of mine. The firework falls on the ground **with a loud explosion as noisy as a car crash.** She gets dizzy and I catch her. My group gets **quiet like they were at a funeral.** One person in my group screams something: "Help, I think she's hurt. . . ." But the adults can't hear. I carry her to my friend's house.

There is silence in the room; she lies on the bed **making minimum moves.** The room filled with teenagers, don't know what to do, wait for the next morning.

30

Personification in Poetry

Focus

Poetry is writing that captures the imagination and the beauty of language in verse. Personification brings imagery to poetry, through the attribution of human qualities to objects, animals, or abstract ideas. During revision, students think about how personification adds imagery and enriches their poetry.

Definitions

Personification: When the writer gives human qualities or characteristics to an animal, idea, or object to create imagery for the reader.

Imagery: Vivid, descriptive words or phrases related to sensory experiences.

Frontloading Activity

Have students listen for personification in poetry as it is read aloud. Any favorite or familiar text can be read. In a local middle school, during the "Poets in the Schools" program of the Pennsylvania Council on the Arts, the late Len Roberts inspired the students with his performance of "The Servant," which includes these lines:

The wind falls, the rain turns the cornstalks

into old men or tomatoes into bleeding soldiers.

Students listen as the teacher reads the poem, "The Servant" by Len Roberts or another favorite poem. They discuss how personification helps to convey imagery for the reader. Then, as a whole class, the students think of human qualities (characteristics, movements, speech) that could apply to animals, ideas, or objects in their everyday lives. Following this activity, students keep a list of these qualities in their writers' notebook. Some examples that students have shared include the following:

- the dancing legs of the piano bench
- the sun smiling down on us
- the whispering winds in the willows

Teaching Tip

Many teachers play music while their students look for examples of personification. Personification abounds in song lyrics as well as poetry.

Procedure

1. Have students write a series of poems over a week.

2. As they share their poetry with their peers, teacher, and parents, they decide on one of their favorite poems to revise. In some classes, students independently make this decision without having shared their poems.

3. Students revise their chosen poems, inserting personification thoughtfully and appropriately (as in the student sample below).

4. Students share their revised poems before they are graded.

An Example of a Student Poem

Lou's final draft

As I Listen

As I sit
on the porch
of the old broken
down house,
I strain to hear
Red robins
yanking
earth worms

from the moist ground.
The air
blows gently,
and in the distance,
I can hear,
A dance of white
butterflies,
Dandelions releasing
Parachutes,
Soldiers marching,
and my mother
calling.

Source: This poem was written as part of the "Poets in the Schools" program of the Pennsylvania Council on the Arts.

31

Write From Another
Point of View

Focus

Students analyze their drafts to identify their own point of view, then attempt to adopt another perspective as they revise. This is a strategy that encourages students to step outside their own writing as they read it, in order to experience their own perspective as another reader might, and then to step into a different point of view as they revise. It's an exercise that requires a good deal of mental flexibility and allows students to improve their skill at revising independently.

Frontloading Activity

Teachers read aloud selections, such as these passages from *Fallen Angels* and *The Lotus Seed*, for students to hear the different points of view from two different characters about the same historical event, in this case, the Vietnam War.

From *Fallen Angels*

"This ain't like Chicago," Monaco said. "They don't kill babies in no Chicago."
    Stewart told us to go to each hut and pick out wounded who looked most like they were going to live and get them ready for evacuation.
    "If you see anybody who looks like a VC make a note of it," he said.
    Body counts. I looked over at Simpson, but he was looking away.

Source: Myers, 2008, pp. 178–179.

From *The Lotus Seed*

My grandmother saw the emperor (of Vietnam) cry the day he lost his golden dragon throne. She wanted something to remember him by so she snuck down to the silent palace, near the River of Perfume, and plucked a seed from a lotus pod that rattled in the Imperial garden.

She hid the seed in a special place under the family altar, wrapped in a piece of silk from the ao dai she wore that day. Whenever she felt sad or lonely, she took out the seed and thought of the brave young emperor.

And when she married a young man chosen by her parents, she carried the seed in her pocket for good luck, long life and many children.

Source: Garland, 1993, p. 2.

Procedure

1. Teachers discuss the war in Vietnam (or another event that provides the backdrop for two selected passages from different perspectives) and how it affected both the soldiers who fought in the war and the Vietnamese people who lived (or didn't) through the war, including the ones who were relocated to the United States, like the characters in *The Lotus Seed*.

2. Teachers describe point of view as the vantage point from which a story is told. In *Fallen Angels*, for example, the point of view is that of the American soldiers following orders from their commanders. In *The Lotus Seed*, the point of view is that of the Vietnamese family determined to make a new home in America.

3. Teachers discuss the advantages of rewriting a draft from a different point of view: to discover new facts, opinions, and experiences related to a topic. For instance, a draft about my grandmother could be written by my sister (her namesake grandchild), my mother (her daughter), and a niece she helped raise. All the drafts would tell the same story but with different experiences, different opinions of my grandmother, and new facts.

4. Students explore other possible points of view for their drafts. The draft could be written from the point of view of another character in the story or a character from outside the story, an observer, or an omniscient, third-party narrator.

5. Students analyze their drafts and find another point of view from which to write their drafts.

6. Students share their different-point-of-view drafts with their peers and discuss which draft they prefer and why.

7. Students decide which point of view provides the most effective story and revise that draft.

PART VII

Digital Communication

Words on Writing From David Lubar

I write on a computer. After I finish my first draft, I print out a copy so I can mark changes on it by hand. Editing on paper feels different from editing on a computer, so I like to do both. I put the changes into the computer file, then keep revising until I'm happy with the whole book. By the time I'm finished, I will probably have gone over the whole book at least eight or ten times. I don't mind—revision is my favorite part of writing.

This final section focuses on how digital tools can support students throughout the revision process. In the strategy *Vocabulary Exploration,* students are given the tools to deepen their vocabulary arsenal and make more informed and conscious decisions about their word choice. Writers are often overwhelmed by the task of selecting and researching a topic—a solitary act that could potentially stop any writing. *Talk Before You Leap is* a revision strategy that incorporates the use of blogs and other digital electronic boards to aid students in their quest for a topic. Similarly, the strategy *Picture This!* illuminates the power of drawing to get inspiration flowing when writer's block hampers a student's writing. In both *Picture This!* and *Talk Before You Leap,* teachers are urged to perform more frontloading activities to support students before they write; as we've emphasized, more frontloading should equal more information and thinking in the prewriting and drafting stages, so less revision is needed.

Writers of all ability levels must attend to syntax and semantic issues in order to craft skillfully designed sentences. In *All Together Now!,* a sentence-combining strategy, the (optional) use of interactive whiteboards can allow students to visualize the task and revise with the touch of a finger or stylus. In many of the revision strategies throughout this book, peer response is a key aspect of activities designed to assist students in revising their own writing. In the revision strategy *Give Me the Highlights!* a free online service called Diigo is used to give all students access to their peers' work and help them give substantial feedback.

Dr. Nanci Werner-Burke, professor at Mansfield University and codirector for the Endless Mountain Writing Project in Mansfield, Pennsylvania, crafted the revision strategies for Part VII.

The Revision Strategies in Part VII Correlated to the 6 Traits of Effective Writing

Strategy/6 Traits	Ideas	Organization	Voice	Word Choice	Sentence Fluency
Vocabulary Exploration	•			•	
Talk Before You Leap	•				
Picture This!	•	•		•	
All Together Now!				•	•
Give Me the Highlights!	•	•		•	

Note: Since the revision strategies do not address Conventions, this trait is not represented in this chart.

32

Vocabulary Exploration

Focus

Through the use of online resources, students deepen their vocabulary arsenal and are able to make conscious and informed decisions about word choices when revising their drafts.

The link between vocabulary knowledge and comprehension is both common sense and supported by research (Barr, Blachowicz, Bates, Katz, & Kaufman, 2006). Students who have a command of more words and their meanings have more choices for communicating ideas and facts with style and clarity.

Writers can acquire new words through reading, writing, listening, and speaking, but learning words consciously and deeply is an incremental process. Teachers should encourage a range of activities that allow students to work with the words in multifaceted settings, drawing on all learning styles, senses, and intelligences. Experimenting with word play can promote the appreciation of language and spark student interest (Graces & Watts-Taffe, 2002), and computer programs that are responsive and interactive can provide the repeated exposures necessary to make the words stick with the reader/writer (Labbo, Love, & Ryan, 2007). The students concentrate on their word choices, which leads to clarification of ideas in their drafts.

The digital tools for this strategy are dictionary and encyclopedia sites, including Visual Thesaurus and Wikipedia.

Frontloading Activities

This strategy works best if the teacher first models how word choice can make one sentence more powerful than another and leads a class discussion during which students experiment with using a variety of words to spice up or clarify a passage. Conversely, Mad Libs can be used to demonstrate how any arbitrary approach to word choice results in awkward, ineffective, or unintentionally hilarious sentences. (Squidoo.com hosts some nice Mad Lib resources.)

Procedure

1. The students exchange working drafts with a peer. They review their partners' drafts to identify words that are used repeatedly or that seem to be vague, plain (depending on the genre), awkward, or incorrectly used. This can be accomplished in rounds, with several students offering feedback.

2. Then the students go online to look up the words targeted by their classmates. Online dictionaries vary in their scope and accessibility. (Looking up *digression* and finding the definition "the act of digressing" doesn't help further a writer's cause much!) The Visual Thesaurus (VT) at www.visualthesaurus.com, however, searches 145,000 English words. While the site charges a fee, it is fairly inexpensive, and students can use it on a trial basis.

3. After using the VT, ask students to decide whether different word choices or other changes might make their drafts more effective. Some students may choose the path of least work; if they report that no changes are needed, they should be asked to support their decisions with examples from the VT. These can be structured by the teacher on accountability slips or can be more open-ended, on post-it notes that the students attach to their drafts.

Teaching Tip

Model the search process on the Visual Thesaurus, drawing attention to the multiple aspects of the site and search results. All the information of a traditional dictionary and thesaurus (definitions, parts of speech) comes up when a term is searched. The strength of this particular online service is that the synonyms are organized in a semantic graphic, that is, by the nature of their relationship to other words.

Demonstrate how students can see the word in context by rolling over it with the mouse and can hear the word spoken aloud by toggling the speaker button.

Go over the color-coding that is used to identify different parts of speech.

Show that if a word that is entered with incorrect spelling, the service suggests a range of alternative spellings. Because of the overlapping, interconnected manner in which the information is presented, the students can easily explore multiple facets of a word.

Variation

Wikipedia (www.wikipedia.org/) is an online service that is still suspect in the eyes of many teachers, since the content on it is open for anyone to contribute to or edit. Contrary to popular belief, however, the content on Wikipedia is mediated to a degree and also poses a unique resource for teaching students to read critically. For word learning, the hyperlink nature of Wikipedia text is valuable in that key words are often clickable, linking the reader/writer to the word in a variety of contexts and definitions; this feature can be used to sharpen understanding of the precise meaning and usage of a term.

Student Example of Vocabulary Exploration

Amy's vocabulary exploration

Amy is writing an informational report on the Holocaust; this is as a frontloading activity to studying the novel *Anne Frank and Me* (Bennett & Gottesfeld, 2001). Amy learned about the battles and leaders of World War II in her history class a few years ago, but she is still struggling with understanding the concept of the Holocaust. She has completed the first two columns of a KWL chart on the subject and used the facts from a few Google searches to frame up a rough draft, but several of the classmates in her writing response group have commented that her use of the term seems vague and fuzzy.

Amy goes to the Visual Thesaurus. (Her school has an online subscription and her teacher has demonstrated how to use the site.) She mistypes the word on her first attempt at searching for related information, and then selects the correct spelling from the options offered by the service (Figure 32.1).

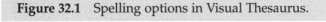

Figure 32.1 Spelling options in Visual Thesaurus.

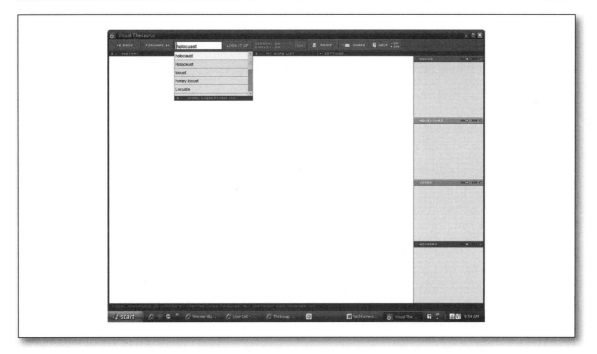

After choosing the correct spelling of the term, Amy's search provides the word map shown in Figure 32.2. Amy clicks on the speaker icon and hears the word spoken aloud. The sound file aligns with how she has been thinking of and pronouncing the word. Next Amy makes a note to ask about the use of a capital *H* that she sometimes sees applied to the term. She sees the phrase "final solution" on the word map and thumbs back to where she has seen this term in her research. She clicks on the word map for more related terms.

Figure 32.2   Word map in Visual Thesaurus.

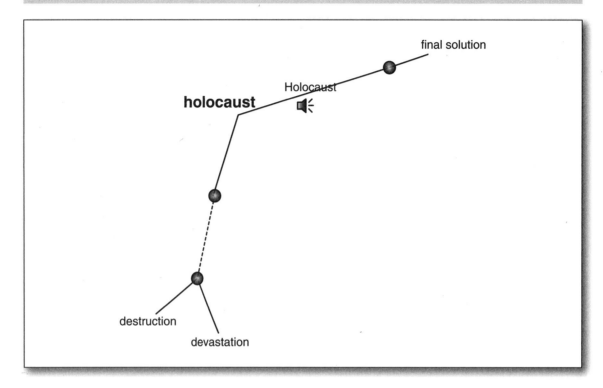

Figure 32.3   Related terms for *Holocaust* as shown in Visual Thesaurus.

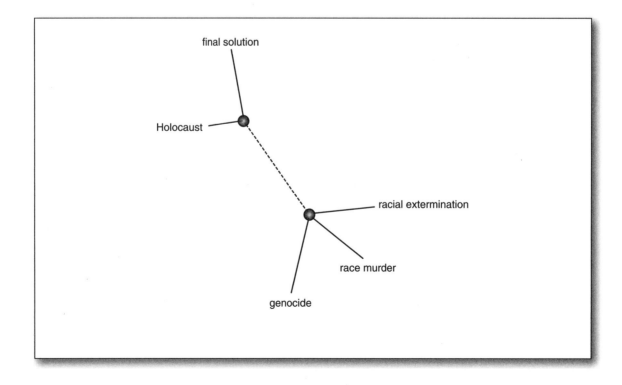

Figure 32.4 Terms generated for Amy's paper by Visual Thesaurus.

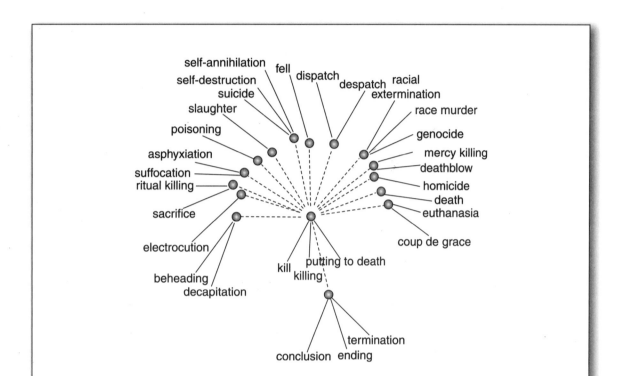

After reading the resulting word map (Figure 32.3), Amy goes back to her rough draft and writes the new terms into the margins. She continues navigating the nodes until she reaches the display in Figure 32.4.

Amy sends the display in Figure 32.4 to herself via her school e-mail account. Later, she prints it and uses a highlighter to pick out terms that she knows from the display that had not been in her original paper or research findings. She also marks the words and phrases she isn't familiar with and adds those to the list of keywords she can use if she gets stuck and needs to do more research.

Eventually, Amy's paper includes many of the terms from Figure 32.4. Reports from her writing group and later from her teacher indicate that the content of her paper is more precise and informative.

33

Talk Before You Leap

Focus

Students often have difficulty choosing topics to research that are both substantial enough for exploration and authentic to them as individuals. When they commit to a topic that is too broad or superficial, the research process can be overwhelming. If they are pressured to commit to a topic that holds little relevance to their personal goals and interests, the process becomes tedious and mechanical for them.

However, when students are encouraged to discuss and defend their topic choices, the process of articulating and explaining helps to focus their efforts and refine their line of inquiry. Allocating time for this frontloading activity helps guide the selection process and reinforces the concept that revision occurs even before the drafting stage.

The late Ken Macrorie introduced the concept of the I-search paper in the late 1980s. In his ground-breaking work, the *I* stood for the actual writer, not for the *information*. The work focused on the value of helping writers choose a viable topic that was authentic. One of the most important facets was that writers kept logs of their self-questioning processes as they poured over different ideas. In effect, the logs show the ongoing revision decisions writers make early on and throughout the process.

Having students use a blog or an electronic message board for this journey is an innovative way for a teacher to make revision more collaborative throughout the entire research process. Two tools they might use include Gaggle and ThinkQuest. Figure 33.1 shows a Gaggle toolbar, and Figure 33.2 shows a sample discussion thread from ThinkQuest.

Teaching Tip

Share a model message with the class before they begin using the discussion boards. There are several examples at the end of this strategy.

Figure 33.1   Gaggle toolbar.

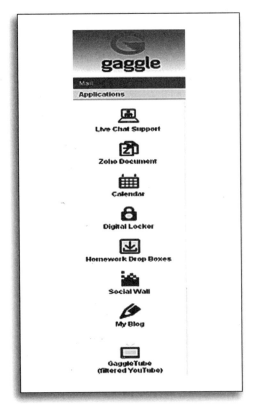

Procedure

1. The teacher reviews the research assignment with the class, including the purpose, audience, format, timeline, and number of required reference sources.

2. The students identify two to three possible topics for the research assignment and outline each of these on a separate message thread on an electronic message/discussion board. Depending on the assignment, the outline must include the following:

   - The topic under consideration
   - For each topic, at least three facets or categories that should be explored
   - Why the writer feels each topic is important and deserving of further investigation, in terms of its relevance to the writer and to the target audience.

3. The students are grouped with four peers on a discussion thread. If multiple classes are working on the same assignment, the groups can be composed of students from different classes.

During group discussion, students are required to review all of the possible topics outlined by their group members and to ask each member a minimum of three questions about the viability and range of his topics. There is no upper limit for questions or suggestions. After responding to the outlines, the group members suggest which topic has the most research potential for each classmate and post the reasons for their choices to the discussion.

Examples of viability and range questions for the minimum wage topic illustrated in Fig. 33.2 might be:

Figure 33.2   A teacher model for a discussion thread as it might look on ThinkQuest.com.

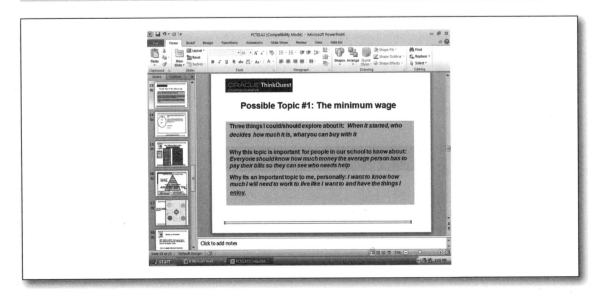

- What do you expect to find?
- What types of sources would you be likely to use in finding this information?
- Will you make a budget based on the minimum wage today? What about one for when it started?
- Is there one minimum wage in the United States? What about other countries?

4. Each student then answers the questions that have been posted by the group and totals the given feedback for each choice. Having the opportunity to retool their topic choices based on the information provided by their peers helps students to move to the next step, which is ranking the topics in terms of potential.

Variations

1. Teachers preassign the group configurations or form groups based on the topics.

2. Groups debate different formats for the project, with the choices being tied to the different topics.

3. Groups are maintained throughout the research assignment. Students add information as they collect it, in subsequent threads. As they engage in their own search for resources, they also share findings on their classmates' topics. This sharing process builds community and can be a precursor to a collaborative group project. It also prepares students to participate in group authorship activities on a wiki.

Teaching Tip

Using Student Message Board Services

Many schools have their own services that they use for digital communication. If your school doesn't subscribe to a service that is set up for student message boards, or if the service is not easy to set up or navigate, you might be tempted to look for a free service for your class to use. Exercise caution, as accounts external to your district can be hard to police, and always get permission before setting up your own board.

When I originally started using e-mail and digital discussion forums with high school students, I used two services: Gaggle.net and Think.com. At that time (2000), Gaggle offered free e-mail services to schools. It has since expanded and now offers e-mail, blogs, message boards, and even texting, though now most schools that use Gaggle pay a subscription fee (about $4-6 per student).

Cropped screenshots of the *Talk Before You Leap* strategy as used by eighth graders on the Gaggle service are shown in Figures 33.3 and 33.4.

ThinkQuest.com (originally Think.com), a free resource for schools (although a signed legal document is necessary), has continued to increase in offerings and ease of use. Through the Think service, students create their own home pages and add limited pictures and links. They also post surveys where classmates and whoever else is on the Think network designated by the teacher cast votes. Discussion groups are easy to format, and for short messages, participants can utilize digital sticky notes. The Think network is handy for setting up exchanges with classrooms across the globe.

Figure 33.3 Students pose their potential topics to classmates.

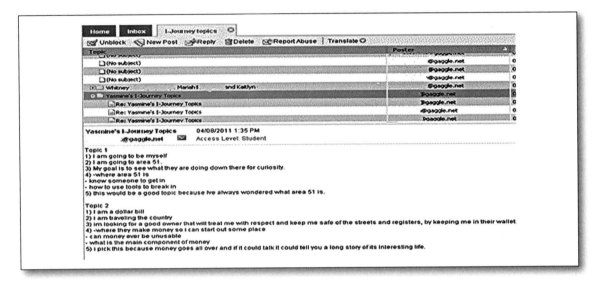

Both services, Gaggle.net and ThinkQuest.com, require formal verification that the participants are affiliated with a school. Schools acknowledge that they are responsible for the actions of their students and that they will not register participants or allow access to individuals who are not staff or students. (This security measure is the reason the students' last names and e-mail accounts do not appear in the examples.) A clear advantage is that the accounts, like a student's locker, belong to the school, with levels of restrictions being within the full control of the district, unlike open forums that pose hazards such as exposure to sexual predators or cyberbullying.

Figure 33.4 Classmates respond and ask additional questions about each topic.

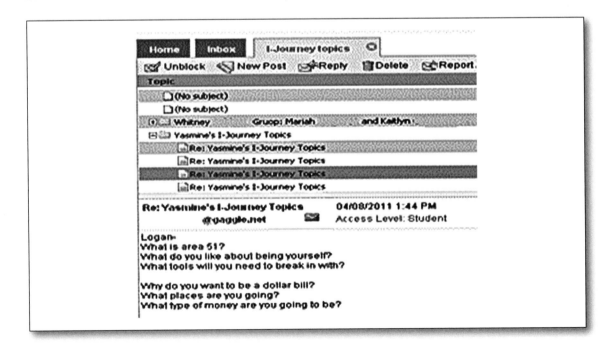

34

Picture This!

Focus

When students hit a wall or get stuck in their writing, ask them to sketch out a scenario related to the idea they are stuck on. Drawn scenarios require writers to think in pictures rather than words, meaning that they are actively visualizing and utilizing different parts of their brains. Details can emerge during the drawing that can later be represented in their drafts or further developed to support their drafts. The shift in the type of directed thinking, moving away from a focus on text, breaks up writer's block.

While there are different ways of comprehending the written word, van den Broek and Kremer emphasize that they all "require readers to create a mental 'picture' of the text, a representation in memory of the text and its interpretation" (2000, p. 2).

Carol Kuhlthau has long studied the social and visual aspects of student research. She notes,

> Organizing ideas graphically is an important strategy for developing thoughts as they are emerging as well as for identifying what is not known and needs to be investigated further in order to be explained. A chart provides a picture of a set of ideas and addresses the connection between the ideas. An outline borders between written discourse and a pictorial depiction of an idea. Charting requires students to create a picture of their thinking. Most young children will readily draw their ideas as a natural expression of their thinking, but as they get older they seem less and less inclined to present their ideas in a pictorial form. It is important to use all of the strategies we have at our disposal to formulate meaning from the abundance of information in digital libraries." (1997, p. 718)

The digital tools for this strategy are the online comic strip and graphic organizer creators Bitstrips and SmartArt.

Procedure

1. In the early stages of organizing and drafting, the teacher shares a short draft of an original piece with the students and discusses how the writer was having trouble moving the piece forward.

2. The teacher shows a visual the writer produced to help her break her writer's block and generate new ideas for the written draft. The visual can be hand drawn or created using Bitstrips (www.bitstripsforschools.com), one of several online comic creators that offers free initial access for schools and individual users.

3. The teacher shares the new ideas the writer generated while creating the visual, and then displays how the writer incorporated these into her draft.

4. Students create a visual for their current work, identify ideas that they generated for their writing while engaged in the drawing activity, and incorporate these into their drafts.

> ## Teaching Tip
>
> While the teacher is the best judge of how much scaffolding students need, this approach lends itself to students with a range of computer and drawing experience, and students have needed little instruction to convert the texts to a graphic format in terms of planning, visualizing, or the actual manipulating of the interface.

Variation

After reviewing a sample text with a whole class, the teacher works with a small group to identify the text structures (process/sequence, compare and contrast relationships, enumeration/list, etc.) that are utilized in the sample. Text structures are the patterns of organization within a passage or written work. The class then uses the SmartArt feature in Microsoft Word and selects a graphic organizer that fits the text structure in the sample.

When students are comfortable with the different structures or patterns, they apply this information to their own work and look for organizational patterns. They choose a graphic organizer template from SmartArt and fill in information from their research notes or data. This approach helps writers to look quantitatively at how they have organized their information and see areas that are under-represented or too detailed and in need of reorganization.

Examples of Students' Bitstrips

Taylor's use of Bitstrips

Figures 34.1 and 34.2 show how Taylor used Bitstrips to create a comic version of an essay she wrote for a scholarship. She commented that the process helped her better understand how she perceived her audience; by selecting the picture of a man in business attire and a top hat to represent the scholarship committee, she then realized that her tone would need to be more formal than that in her first draft. Choosing the background for the last two frames helped her to realize that she wanted the scholarship to help her make the shift from a high school world to one where she was actively earning money and taking on the financial responsibilities of adult life. She also titled her work, because there was a specific place to do so on Bitstrips; whereas, it had not occurred to her to create a title in her written work before this activity.

Figure 34.1   Taylor's first comic version of her scholarship essay.

Figure 34.2   Graphic organizer for use with Bitstrips.

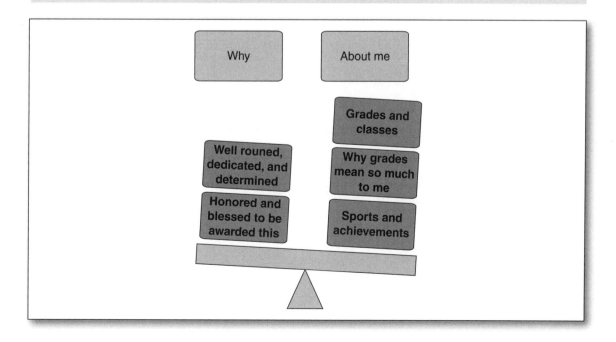

After organizing her essay into the graphic organizer in Figure 34.2, Taylor decided her draft was more focused on her activities than on reasons why she should be awarded the scholarship. She revised her paper to better reflect a balance between the two ideas.

Alyssa's use of Bitstrips

Figures 34.3 and 34.4 show how Alyssa used a graphic organizer to group her information into categories, which she then further revised into questions.

Figure 34.3   Bitstrip initially created by Alyssa.

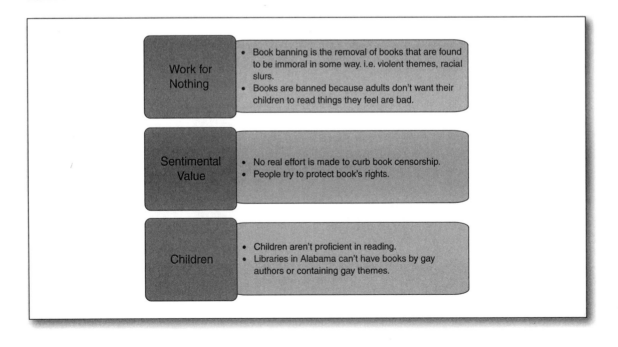

Figure 34.4   The graphic organizer for Alyssa's Bitstrip.

35

All Together Now!

Focus

While longer sentences aren't necessarily better (consider the brevity of "To be or not to be"), when students have strategies to combine multiple sentences into more cohesive thoughts, they have more options in their writing toolkit. In addition, when source sentences are not of high quality, students need strategies to become aware of issues with syntax and semantics at both the sentence and passage level.

Sentence combining is a well-documented, effective way to help K–12 students develop the skills they need to create mature sentences of their own (Saddler, 2007). Good digital tools for this strategy are readily available in Microsoft Word and other word-processing programs in the form of word-counting features, and when interactive whiteboards, such as Promethean or SMART boards, are available, the process literally puts the writer in a hands-on situation in the middle of a text.

Procedure

1. The teacher models ways to combine two or more sentences through a think-aloud, involving the class in the discussion and in making the choices, which are projected for the students to see.

2. The students are given two or more sentences with related thoughts and asked to combine them into one. In pairs, the students explore a variety of options before deciding which combination of sentences they feel is best in terms of syntax and communication.

3. The student pairs share their answers with the class, explaining what they thought was not clear or correct about the original sentences and what the sentences had in common so that they could be effectively combined.

Teaching Tip/Variation: Using Interactive Whiteboards

An interactive whiteboard (SMART, Promethean, etc.) can be extremely helpful classroom tool. Much like standard dry erase boards in appearance, interactive whiteboards are designed to function as giant touch screens. The Promethean brand provides a special stylus for these purposes, and SMART boards allow one to touch using a finger.

Initially, the interactive whiteboard is often used for modeling the sentence-combining approach and for supporting student engagement when demonstrating the strategy. The entire class can view the content and participate. The students can move parts of the text with their fingers or the stylus, making the process at once both physical and virtual. When used to teach the *All Together Now!* revision strategy, this technology allows teachers to differentiate instruction based on their students' strengths and needs and to more clearly understand students' thinking processes as they approach a text.

In the early stages, teachers should consider selecting passages from writers external to the classroom writing community. It's typically easier for student writers to revise such an external text, because they don't have to attend to the writer's feelings. As they develop confidence and competency with the skill, they can then apply it in revision groups and when looking at their own work.

An additional tool that can make it easy for teachers to implement this approach is the optical character recognition (OCR) feature available on most scanners. This tool scans paragraphs into a word-processing program for students to practice the revision strategy. Rather than converting a text into a picture or photo file, the OCR function recognizes the actual letters and scans them individually, creating a digital version that students can revise and edit. This is useful for a sentence-combining strategy and a myriad of other teaching strategies.

An Example of Student Revision

Original paragraph from an external source

Gorilla meat is a dietary staple for nearly 12 million people who live near the rainforests of central and West Africa. Some Africans prefer bush meat, such as gorilla, because it provides an economical source of daily protein. Poor families without the means to purchase food at the market travel a short distance to the rainforest to get bush meat. Their only expense is the cost of ammunition and the fee to rent a gun. Some of these same families raise chickens and goats, but do not eat them. Instead, they sell the animals for the cash they need for buying supplies. Africa's population is increasing rapidly, along with its demand for bush meat. If nothing changes, primatologists fear that gorillas may become extinct in the next thirty years.

Source: Gorillas in Crisis by Kathleen Donovan-Snavely, 2004. Retrieved from the Read Write Think database: http://www .readwritethink.org/lesson_images/lesson277/gorillas.pdf

Jessica's revision

Figure 35.1 Summarizing and sentence-combining passage written by Jessica.

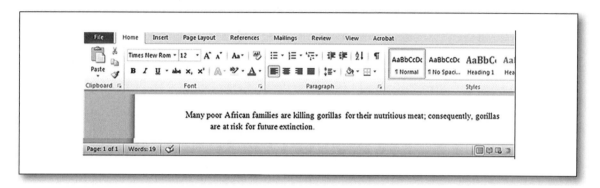

Many poor African families are killing gorillas for their nutritious meat; consequently, gorillas are at risk for future extinction.

36

Give Me the Highlights!

Focus

During peer conferencing, we ask writers to read and mark up drafts created by their classmates, as a means of providing direction for revisions. When members of the peer response group are limited in their own reading capabilities or experiences, the quality and utility of their feedback suffers. Through directed highlighting and annotating, students can begin to access the nuances of meaning and larger patterns of organization. Online services for educators, such as Diigo, can be used for this purpose.

Zywica and Gomez (2008) note that annotation is a structured way for students to mark up their drafts so they are more manageable. It helps readers begin to analytically approach texts by looking for structures and patterns that are used to convey information, and it helps them make connections and contexts visible. Annotation encourages students to debate correct main ideas and supporting ideas, which in turn means they are learning the foundational skills for debate and argument through talking and analyzing.

For many teachers, making copies of readings for students to physically write on can be a hindrance to having students practice marking up texts and making annotation (Zywica & Gomez, 2008). This is true for student work as well as for traditional textbooks. One solution to the paper crunch is for students to work with digital texts using digital mark-up and commentary tools. When writers are taught to become active readers who interact critically with text, the benefit is manifested in increased reading power across contexts and improved feedback for revision on their peers' drafts.

Teaching Tip

The teacher should consider the following when deciding whether this approach will be useful for the class:

- Has the group worked with peer feedback on written work previously and had difficulty generating specific, useful feedback for classroom authors?
- Has the teacher observed or documented struggles with reading comprehension in the class?

If the answer to either question is affirmative, the teacher should consider applying a variation of this strategy.

Procedure

1. Set up accounts for the class members using the free Diigo service (www.diigo.com). Diigo has special accounts for educators. Once you have confirmed with Diigo that you are a teacher (and you have the permission of your IT personnel and building administrators to move forward), you will be able to log in and set up accounts for your class. Split the class into groups of four or five and set up the groups in Diigo so that all members in a group have access to each other's information.

2. Select the text each group will be working with online. Ideally, the selected texts will be well written, of interest to the age group, strongly related to content in their curriculum or areas of study, accessible in terms of language used and clarity, and of a length that the group will be able to work with during one class period. The members of a group will all be working with the same text for the activity.

3. Form students into groups and assign them an article to read, and give each group member a response role to fulfill. That role dictates what facet of the writing each student is to focus on initially when reading the article. The nature of actual roles can vary according to the mode and structure of the actual text passage, but the following framework, which is often used to analyze and develop the trait of voice in writing (Dean, 2006), provides a solid basis for implementing this approach:

   - Diction: Word choice of the author.
   - Images: Author's evocation of sensory ideas.
   - Detail: Author's choice of individual details to share.
   - (Figurative) Language: The style of language the author chooses, including jargon, colloquialisms, and so forth that denote a location, time period, and more.
   - Syntax: The way an author chooses to arrange words and utilize conventions to convey ideas.

4. Project a sample text on a screen and model examples of each of the response roles for the class; then project a second text and engage the class in identifying where each of roles could come into play.

5. The class then moves into their groups and logs in to Diigo with the user name and password you have supplied for them. They'll need to download and install the Diigo toolbar, pictured in Figure 36.1 in a screenshot from the Diigo website that shows the toolbar and corresponding labels for each feature.

6. Once the students have logged in and activated the toolbar, they access the online article with which they will be working. The group should read the article aloud, either by taking turns or by having one or two members volunteer. The group then turns their individual efforts toward marking up the text in accordance with their assigned response roles, through highlighting relevant portions and annotating them, noting how the highlighted text corresponds with the role. It's useful to correlate each responsive role with a different highlighting color.

7. The students in the group read, highlight, and comment in accordance with their roles; then they comment on the work of their classmates in the group. The group works together to evaluate the article in accordance with the roles and to formulate affirmation and advice for the author. The initial commentary should be limited to correspondence with the roles. After each role has been examined, comments may address other areas of the writing.

Figure 36.1 The Diigo toolbar.

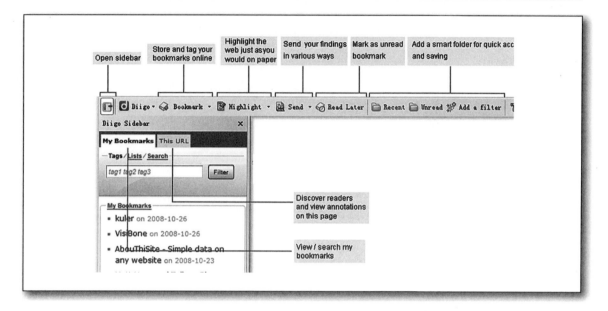

8. Then the students reconvene as a whole class and share what they have done with their articles, using the projection screen.

9. Eventually, students use these skills to respond to the work of their peers. After practicing this strategy, students often offer more pointed, specific feedback to their peers on their drafts.

Teaching Tip

Roles within a group can be modified to fit a larger instructional objectives and curricular focus. Fisher, Brozo, Frey, and Ivey (2011) suggest the following roles for facilitating reciprocal teaching, all of which can be used to help students interact with a text via structured annotation:

- Summarizing
- Questioning
- Clarifying
- Predicting

When the target text is in narrative form, the literature circle roles in the list below can be used. Note that the literature circle framework list includes an external role of group monitor, which may be a useful option depending on the students in the class.

- Discussion Director: Creates questions to increase comprehension.
- Vocabulary Enricher: Clarifies word meanings and pronunciations.
- Literary Luminary: Examines figurative language, parts of speech, and vivid descriptions.
- Checker: Helps monitor discussion for equal participation.

Figure 36.2 Text in Diigo marked up by three students.

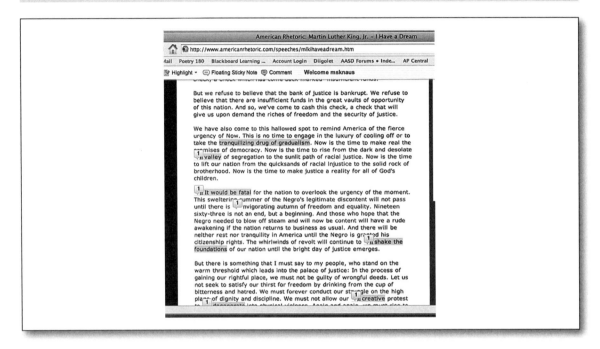

An Example of Student Work

Figure 36.2 shows a text in Diigo in which the highlighter tool has been used by three high school students to collaboratively read and mark up a text. The students used the sticky note tool to explain their reasons for highlighting (Figure 36.3).

Figure 36.3 The same text showing sticky note annotations.

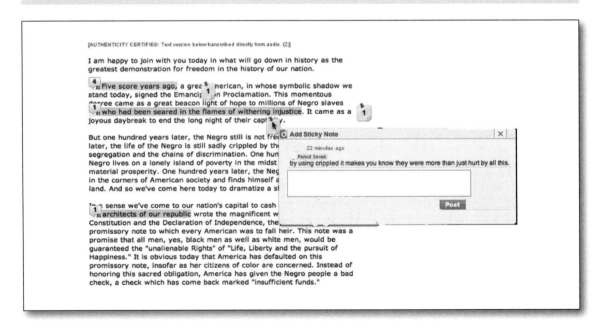

References and Further Reading

Anderson, L. H. (1999). *Speak.* New York, NY: Penguin.

Anderson, L. H. (2010). *Chains.* New York, NY: Simon & Schuster.

Atwell, N. (1987*). In the middle: Writing, reading, and learning with adolescents.* Portsmouth, NH: Heinemann.

Barr, R., Blachowicz, C., Bates, A., Katz, C., & Kaufman, B. (2006). *Reading diagnosis for teachers: An instructional approach.* New York, NY: Allyn & Bacon.

Bennett, C., & Gottesfeld, J. (2001). *Anne Frank and me.* New York, NY: Putnam's.

Biancarosa, C., & Snow, C. E. (2006). *Reading next—A vision for action and research in middle and high school literacy: A report to Carnegie Corporation of New York* (2nd ed.).Washington, DC: Alliance for Excellent Education.

Borgese, J. (1998*). A correlation study of the West Chester School District's writing assessment and standardized test scores of sophomores.* Chester, PA: Widener University.

Burke, J. (2003). *Writing reminders: Tools, tips, and techniques.* Portsmouth, NH: Heinemann.

Cisneros, S. (1991). *House on Mango Street.* New York, NY: Vintage.

Claggett, F., Brown, J., Reid, L., & Patterson, N. (2005). *Teaching writing: Art, craft, genre.* Urbana, IL: National Council of Teachers of English.

Culham, R. (2003). *6 + 1 traits of writing: The complete guide (Grade 3 and up).* New York, NY: Scholastic.

Curtis, C. P. (1995). *The Watsons go to Birmingham—1963.* New York, NY: Dell Books.

Dean, N. (2006). *Discovering voice: Voice lessons for middle and high school.* Gainesville, FL: Maupin House.

Dickson, D., Heyler, D., Reilly, L., & Romano, S. (2006). *The oral history project: Connecting students to their community, grades 4–8.* Portsmouth, NH: Heinemann.

Diederich, P. (1974). *Measuring growth in English.* Urbana, IL: National Council of Teachers of English.

Dorfman, L., & Cappelli, R. (2009). *Nonfiction mentor texts: Teaching informational writing through children's literature, K–8.* Portland, ME: Stenhouse.

Elbow, P., & Belanoff, P. (1999). *A community of writers: A workshop course in writing* (3rd ed.). Columbus, OH: McGraw-Hill.

Faigley, L., & Witte, S. (1981). Analyzing revision. *College Composition, 32,* 400–410.

Fink, L. S. (n.d.). *Literature circles: Getting started.* Retrieved from http://www.readwritethink.org/classroom-resources/lesson-plans/literature-circles-getting-started-19.html

Fisher, D., Brozo, W., Frey, N., & Ivey, G. (2011). *50 instructional routines to develop content literacy.* Upper Saddle River, NJ: Pearson/Merrill.

Fox, M. (1985). *Wilfrid Gordon McDonald Partridge.* La Jolla, CA: Kane/Miller.

Gaines, E. J. (1997). *A lesson before dying.* New York, NY: Vintage.

Gallagher, K. (2006). *Teaching adolescent writers.* Portland, ME: Stenhouse.

Garland, S. (1993). *The lotus seed.* San Diego, CA : Harcourt Brace Jovanovich.

Goldberg, N. (2005). *Writing down the bones: Freeing the writer within.* Boston, MA: Shambhala.

Graces, M., & Watts-Taffe, S. M. (2002). The place of word consciousness in a research-based vocabulary program. In A. Farstrup (Ed.), *What the research has to say about reading instruction* (pp. 140–165). Newark, DE: International Reading Association.

Graves, D. H. (1983). *Writing: Teachers & children at work.* Portsmouth, NH: Heinemann.

Graves, D. H. (2004). *Teaching day by day: 180 stories to help you along the way.* Portsmouth, NH: Heinemann.

Graves, D. H., & Kittle, P. (2005). *Inside writing: How to teach the details of craft.* Portsmouth, NH: Heinemann.

Hansberry, L. (2004). *A raisin in the sun.* New York, NY: Vintage.

Head, A., & Eisenberg, M. (2010). *Truth be told: How college students evaluate and use information in the digital age.* Project Information Literacy project report. Retrieved from http://projectinfolit.org/pdfs/PIL_Fall2010_Survey_FullReport1.pdf

Heard, G. (2002). *The revision toolbox: Teaching techniques that work.* Portsmouth, NH: Heinemann.

Hicks, T. (2009). *The digital writing workshop.* Portsmouth, NH: Heinemann.

Hoyt, L. (2000). *Snapshots: Literacy minilessons up close.* Portsmouth, NH: Heinemann.

Kidd, S. M. (2001). *The secret life of bees.* New York, NY: Penguin.

Kirby, D., Kirby, D. L., & Liner, T. (2004). *Inside out: Strategies for teaching writing.* Portsmouth, NH: Heinemann.

Korman, G. (2010). *Framed.* New York, NY: Scholastic.

Kuhlthau, C. C. (1997). Learning in digital libraries: An information search process approach. *Library Trends, 45,* 708–724. Retrieved from http://www.ideals.illinois.edu/bitstream/handle/2142/8113/library trendsv45i4k_opt.pdf?sequence=1

L' Engle, M. (2007). *A wrinkle in time.* New York, NY: Houghton Mifflin Harcourt.

Labbo, L., Love, M. S., and Ryan, T. (2007). A vocabulary flood: Making words "sticky" with computer-response activities. *The Reading Teacher, 60*(6), 582–588.

Lamb, W. (2000). *The hour I first believed.* New York, NY: HarperCollins.

Lane, B. (1993). *After the end: Teaching and learning creative revision.* Portsmouth, NH: Heinemann.

Lane, B. (2008). *But how do you teach writing? A simple guide for all teachers.* New York, NY: Scholastic Teaching Resources.

Law, I. (2008). *Savvy.* New York, NY: Penguin.

Lee, H. (1960). *To kill a mockingbird.* New York, NY: HarperCollins.

Lewis, C. S. (1978). *The lion, the witch, and the wardrobe.* New York, NY: HarperCollins.

Louth, R. (2010). *A guide for writing marathon leaders.* Retrieved from http://www.nwp.org/cs/public/print/resource/3162

Lowry, L. (1989). *Number the stars.* New York, NY: Farrar, Straus & Giroux.

Macrorie, K. (1988). *The I-search paper.* Portsmouth, NH: Boynton/Cook.

Murray, D. (1982). *Learning by teaching.* Portsmouth, NH: Heinemann.

Murray, D. (1995). *The craft of revision.* Orlando, FL: Harcourt Brace College Publishers.

Myers, W. D. (2008). *Fallen angels.* New York, NY: Scholastic.

Namioka, L. (2000). *Ties that bind, ties that break.* New York, NY: Laurel Leaf.

National Commission on Writing. (2006). *Writing and school reform and the neglected "r": The need for a writing revolution.* Retrieved from http://www.collegeboard.com/prod_downloads/writingcom/neglectedr.pdf

O'Dell, S. (2010). *Island of the blue dolphins.* New York, NY: Houghton Mifflin.

Patterson, K. (2003). *Bridge to Terabithia.* New York, NY: HarperCollins.

Paulsen, G. (2007). *Hatchet.* New York, NY: Simon & Schuster.

Pennsylvania Department of Education Bureau of Assessment and Accountability. (2008–2009). *The Pennsylvania System of School Assessment, Grade 7, Reading Item and Scoring Sampler.* Harrisburg, PA: Author. Available from http://www.portal.state.pa.us

Quindlen, A. (1997). *One true thing.* New York, NY: Delta.

Rawls, W. (1997). *Where the red fern grows.* Evanston, IL: McDougal Littell.

Roberts, L. (2001). *The silent singer: New and selected poems.* Champaign: University of Illinois Press.

Routman, R. (2004). *Writing essentials: Raising expectations and results while simplifying teaching.* Portsmouth, NH: Heinemann.

Ryan, P. M. (2002). *Esperanza rising.* New York, NY: Scholastic.

Saddler, B. (2007). Improving sentence construction skills through sentence combining practice. In S. Graham, C. A. MacArthur, & J. Fitzgerald (Eds.), *Best practices in writing instruction* (pp. 163–178). New York, NY: The Guilford Press.

Sapphire. (1997). *Push.* New York, NY: Vintage.

Schlink, B. (1999). *The reader.* New York, NY: Vintage.

Sebold, A. (2004). *Lovely bones.* New York, NY: Back Bay Books.

Sebranek, P., Kemper, D., & Meyer, V. (2006). *Writers INC: A student handbook for writing and learning.* Wilmington, MA: Great Source Education Group.

Sebranek, P., Kemper, D., & Meyer, V. (2010). *Write on course: A student handbook for writing, thinking, and learning.* Orlando, FL: Great Source Education Group.

Sebranek, P., Meyer, V., & Kemper, D. (2007). *Write for college.* Wilmington, MA: Great Source Education Group.

Selznick, B. (2007). *The invention of Hugo Cabret.* New York, NY: Scholastic.

Spandel, V. (2009). *Creating 6-trait revisers and editors for grade 8.* Boston, MA: Pearson.

Spandel, V., & Stiggins, R. J. (2009). *Creating writers: Linking writing assessment and instruction* (5th ed.). New York, NY: Addison Wesley Longman.

Spinelli, J. (2003). *Milkweed.* New York, NY: Random House.

Spinelli, J. (2007). *Eggs.* New York, NY: Little Brown.

van den Broek, P., & Kremer, K. (2000). The mind in action: What it means to comprehend during reading. In B. Taylor, M. S. Graves, & P. van den Broek (Eds.), *Reading for meaning: Fostering comprehension in the middle grades* (pp. 1–31). New York, NY: Teachers College Press.

VanderMey, R., Meyer, V., Van Rys, J., Kemper, D., & Sebranek, P. (2004). *The college writer: A guide to thinking, writing, and researching.* Boston, MA: Houghton Mifflin.

Whyte, P. (2006, July 31). *DIDLS.* Presentation at the College Board's AP Summer Institute—English Literature and Composition. Rensselaerville, NY.

Willis, M. (1993). *Deep revision: A guide for teachers, students, and other writers.* New York, NY: Teachers & Writers Collaborative.

Zywica, J., & Gomez, K. (2008). Annotating to support learning in the content areas: Teaching and learning science. *Journal of Adolescent & Adult Literacy, 52*(2), 155.

Index

Pages followed by f indicate figures

CORWIN
A SAGE Company

The Corwin logo—a raven striding across an open book—represents the union of courage and learning. Corwin is committed to improving education for all learners by publishing books and other professional development resources for those serving the field of PreK–12 education. By providing practical, hands-on materials, Corwin continues to carry out the promise of its motto: **"Helping Educators Do Their Work Better."**